Easy, Everyday Habits
To Be More
eco-friendly

My personal journey easing back into a sustainable life
and how you can, too.

Amanda Gates

Easy, Everyday Habits
To Be More
eco-friendly

1

Why small steps to being eco-friendly matters.
even if you have to use paper plates.

2

What exactly does eco-friendly look like?

3

Seeing Green. Simple solutions start at home.

4

How to reduce your carbon footprint.
even if you have no idea who carbon is.

5

Everyday habits start with you.

Easy, Everyday Habits
To Be More
eco-friendly

6

How to ease into a zero waste life.

7

Random acts of sustainability.

8

Seeing green. how to bring it all together as a lifestyle.

9

PS: Additional resources to be a sustainable rockstar.

"Be kind, be generous and love Mama Earth like the wise, loving grandmother She is."

amanda gates

66

What does eco look like?

YOU.

ONE

WHY SMALL STEPS TO BEING ECO-FRIENDLY MATTERS, EVEN IF YOU HAVE TO USE PAPER PLATES.

LISTEN, sometimes being green isn't easy, but it's important to remember to not be too hard on yourself, because it's certainly not impossible but absolutely necessary. A lot of good comes from every sustainable practice, no matter how small it is, even if you're simultaneously using a few paper plates along the way. Life can be challenging at times so it's easy to get swept up in our modern day conveniences that make life easier. When I was in high school, we used paper plates for everything. When Mom was raising us kids, she worked 60+ hours a week and life was busy, but it wasn't always that way.

Before she met my stepdad, I was always the weird kid at school. Why? Well, no matter how hard I tried to fit in, mom was always right behind me throwing down landmines making my life as unbearable as she possibly could. I swear she gained the greatest pleasure from my awkward, disjointed childhood.

At lunch I didn't have the cool Lunchables, or preservative-laden chips covered in cheese like Doritos. I was the lucky winner of homemade granola, veggie slices and a side salad. Meanwhile, Misty, the most popular girl in school, got the pizza rolls, Cheetos and a Coke for lunch! Man was I jealous.

To make matters worse, mom made all of my clothes too. We

would head down to the fabric store and she'd use every last scrap making me a shirt, matching pants, a headband and anything else in between to make sure no scrap was left behind. I was told daily that I was "lucky" because the other kids had to wear store-bought clothes. And if I groaned about the homemade clothes, she'd march my butt down to Leroy's thrift store where we'd spend hours scouring through all the racks to find the best deals on the best clothes for the upcoming school year.

Shoot me now I'd think. All I wanted to do was shop at Miller's Outpost, because that's where Misty bought all her clothes. If I could shop there I could buy new Levi's and a new, mass produced shirt. Or maybe some cute cut-off jeans with bows cut out on the side. But noooo, mom wanted to be weird, and the buck didn't stop with her. Grandma was weird too. What I couldn't understand was why we shopped and lived like poor people. We had plenty of money so why were we spending days making our own yogurt, growing our own fruit to can for winter and shopping at thrift stores? God we were so weird, and boy did I have a lot to learn!

These weird, AKA sustainable, ways went on for years until my mom remarried in the early nineties. Things changed quickly and to my delight, life turned normal! We built a new home, mom started working more and my stepdad's kids moved in with us. Mom got so busy she started giving me money for school lunch (for the love of all things good there is a God!), and I was finally decked out in all things mass produced and cool. I was a sophomore in high school and blended in to the herd of eco-sucking, unsustainable teenagers, and I couldn't be happier.

It's funny, when I look back at those formidable years, all I wanted to do was fit in. I desperately wanted to blend in and be cool - even if that meant sacrificing the planet. I mean seriously, if it meant stabbing the planet right in the left eye or being a trash producing, eco-sucking, unsustainable teenager, I would hands down choose the stupid teenager any day of the week. I mean this was high school and fitting in was important, right?

Fast forward to me today, not only have I surpassed my eco-loving mother, but I have felt it my civic responsibility to be an advocate for this planet and teach everything I know. I proudly shop at thrift stores, make my own cleaners, make everything from scratch, reuse, reduce and recycle everything, and will gladly be *weird* if it helps save Mama Earth.

Now you may be saying to yourself, well sure, you can do it, but my little *things* won't matter. I understand the thinking, but that's where you're wrong and here's why. I often felt like it was an all or nothing game. That I was a hypocrite if my entire life wasn't absolutely "green." How could I tell people to do all these things when I myself would forget to put out my own recycling or use a paper plate? Luckily, mom stepped in to save us all.

Here's the real truth direct from mom, "it's not an all or nothing game." The truth is simple, we are killing our planet at an alarming rate. In only fifty years we have consumed more resources than in our entire existence. This is no longer a matter of "if" but a matter of "when," and if we continue at the current rate we are going, our planet will be destroyed in 100 short years.

Our culture thrives on consumption and the more we are fed the more we buy. So where does one even start? Here's the takeaway; we can no longer place our head in the sand. This is arguably one of the most important topics that few are even taking into consideration, because so many think they can't make a difference. But doing a few simple things every day does in fact make big impacts, especially if everyone (there are seven billion people on this planet) takes action.

So, you may be saying, "Ok, great, but what does it mean to be sustainable?" Sustainable living means that you are proactive in reducing your demand on resources. In other words, you're making conscious decisions when you replace what you use, or items you need, to the best of your ability, with an eco solution. For example, making a choice not to consume a product that isn't made with sustainability in mind. Or it means changing how you do everyday things so that you become an active participant in the cycle of renewing life.

Unless you've been living under a rock, most already know that climate change, global warming, and depletion of resources are real and their impact, if ignored, will be devastating. Even if you can't do 20 things every day this is an opportunity for you to learn how to adopt two or three easy practices for a more sustainable life. Endorsing this way of living helps reduce your carbon footprint and environmental impact, which we will talk more about in an upcoming chapter.

Here's the rub; simple measures like reducing your energy consumption by using more eco-friendly lights, using public transportation once or twice a week, choosing to not eat meat regularly, or buying second hand when replacing an item, can go a long way in reducing your environmental imprint on this planet, ultimately making this planet a clean and safe place to live. Your purchases equal a vote, so the more you buy the more you say YES to consumption of unsustainable resources.

This misconception that sustainability is an all or nothing kind of game is nonsense. Sustainability and helping the environment starts with awareness. Simply paying attention to your everyday decisions is a step in the right direction. Being sustainable will look different for everyone, but the environment and your daily habits need to be at the top of the list. And here's the good news: the tips included in this book are easy to adopt, easy to implement and before you know it you'll be a bonafide hippie!

You carry Mother Earth within you. She is not outside of you. Mother Earth is not just your environment. In that insight of inter-being, it is possible to have real communication with the Earth, which is the highest form of prayer. Thich Nhat Hanh

 Eco Facts

17
Years of expected life span for the average LED bulb.

8 Billion gallons of gas saved if every commuter took two people to work.

330
Gallons of water saved if one person used a high efficiency toilet for one year.

Less than 20% of plastic bottles are actually recycled, use glass instead.

50
Amount of years that humans have consumed more resources than in all previous history.

26 Despite accounting for only 5% of the world's population, Americans consume 26% of the world's energy.

Coal   Oil   Gas   Nuclear   Hybrid   Other

"

refuse what you do not need; reduce what you do need; reuse what you consume; recycle what you cannot refuse and rot the rest

Bea Johnson
author
Zero Waste Home

Chapter 1

Radical eco thoughts

1

Can you think of little practices that you're already doing daily
that make a big difference?

2

Do you consider yourself an eco-friendly person?

3

What does eco-friendly look and feel like to you?

4

What do you expect eco-friendly to look like
after reading this book?

5

What can you do without in the next 30 days?
Coffee in paper cups, plastic utensils, bottled water, straws?

Radical eco thoughts

Notes:

Radical eco thoughts

Notes:

TWO

WHAT EXACTLY DOES ECO-FRIENDLY LOOK LIKE?

BEING eco-friendly has become quite trendy, so much so that a term called "greenwashing" has evolved from it. You can find it in everything from job ads to dating profiles, home listings to every type of consumer product imaginable. If you're just starting out, dipping your toe into this uncharted abyss, it can be easy to fall prey to glossy marketing traps. Remember, your dollar equals a vote.

First, in order to be eco-friendly, you have to become aware of how your choices and decisions affect the environment. There are four basic principles to take into consideration:

1) How can you reduce the items you currently consume? For example, do you really need ten toiletries?

2) Choose to consume only items that cause minimal to no environmental harm, like 50% post-consumer products, used goods or repurposed goods.

3) Understand the extent of your carbon footprint and choose to lessen that footprint on the environment every day.

4) Support others that live and work to produce eco-friendly and sustainable products, communities and lifestyles.

In the last 100 years consumerism has quadrupled. We have been led to believe that more is more and that coveting or having an inordinate amount of things is the path to happiness. Getting and spending fills the desire for a truly meaningful life.

We live in a world of mass production: clothes, furniture, toys, cars, food - all produced and manufactured in big ass factories that tax the hell out of our natural resources. Since most of us never participate in the actual making of these consumable items, we tend to take their very existence for granted because they magically appear on the shelves of our ubiquitous superstores and presumably make our lives better. Tada!

So when asked the question, "What exactly does being eco-friendly look like?" It looks like you. The first question requires you to be honest about the way you consume and immediately act in changing it. The average woman spends $150 each month on toiletries alone.

Think about the resources involved with the packaging produced, the chemicals that go down the drain and the dollars wasted. This means it's time to have a come-to-Jesus meeting with yourself about what you really need versus want. In other words, changing your habits around what types of packaging you use, where you buy your goods, how you buy your goods and how you dispose of waste.

It's easy to throw your hands up in the air, but I promise you're going to walk away from this book with tangible tips to nail this eco-friendly stuff. As mom used to always say, "you've gotta pick your battles." By the time I got into high school, mom was raising three kids, working full time and also taking care of my dad who just got hurt at work.

To say things were hectic for her was an understatement. To make her life easier we started using paper plates. Was she happy about it? Not in the least. But with five people in the house and no dishwasher, Mom could no longer keep up, and there will be times you'll do the same.

Life fluctuates, ebbs and flows. When things get really hectic, don't be hard on yourself. Do the best that you can and just be aware that every little bit helps. Even if you can only do one or two things, you're making a difference. I promise.

My high school years are a bit of a blur for Mom. She had a lot on her paper plate and she was forced to pivot. The good news is, she had been eco-friendly her entire life, so I don't think Mama Earth held her responsible for the few years she felt she was spinning in twenty directions.

Even though we converted to paper plates, we still continued to sit down every night for dinner as a family. She continued to can fruit, albeit not as much as she used to, make everything from scratch, make her own soaps and occasionally she'd even sew a dress for my prom or homecoming.

The sustainability never left her, it just got a little distracted, and that brings me to number two on our list: If you must consume, choose items with a low environmental impact.

66 The word consumption increasingly lost its earlier connotations of destroying, wasting, or using up, and came instead to refer in a positive way to the satisfying of human needs and desires.

Stephanie Coontz, The Way We Were: American Families and The Nostalgia Trap 99

Despite Mom becoming incredibly busy in my later years she still managed to stay true to her eco-friendly heart. Even though she wasn't doing fifty things, she still managed to do ten things pretty regularly. One such example was that she still shopped at thrift stores and she was the queen of getting ten uses out of one item.

Remember, it's not an all or nothing game, everything counts. Mom used to always say, if you do ten things and twenty people you know do ten things, the outcome really starts to add up, and she's right. It's not about loud, gregarious roars but subtle everyday actions combined with other small actions that add up to big environmental reward.

I think the trick to being more environmentally conscious is looking at it in a different way. When I started easing back into sustainable practices I didn't decide to do twenty things all at once.

After my divorce I started to slowly educate myself on what being sustainable looked like for me. As you start to take action in becoming more eco- friendly your biggest task each day will be determining what eco-friendly looks like to you. Do you really need to buy a coffee at Starbucks when there's coffee at home? Four billion Starbucks cups go into landfills annually. Your dollar is a vote, so choose to consume wisely.

Case in point: Reusable produce bags are a great place to start. On average I discovered I was using ten plastic produce bags per trip to the store. Going once a week to the store I was contributing forty plastic bags going into landfills per month, just so I could bring my veggies home on a short, five minute drive home. Even if I forget my bags 50% of the time I'm still preventing close to 250 bags each year from going into landfills. And that brings me to principle three: What is the extent of your carbon footprint?

How can you act with responsibility to lessen that imprint to the best of your ability?

Although seemingly small, I gifted five of my family members reusable produce bags. This was a conscious decision on my part to decrease my footprint along with the people around me.

Assuming they forgot their bags half of the time, they are still saving over 1200 bags a year from going into landfills. And if they made a conscious effort to NOT forget they saved 2500 bags a year from going in landfills. Now just think about that for a moment. Think about every person on this planet putting their fruits and veggies in a plastic bag just simply to bring them home. That's a huge tax on our environment for the sake of convenience.

Now consider this. I've been using my reusable produce bags for about five years now. On average, reusable bags have a lifespan that saves over 1700+ plastic bags from going into landfills. The average person uses between 300-500 plastic bags every single year!

One person making the conscious effort of using reusable bags can save nearly 20,000 bags from going into landfills in their lifetime. Plus, what most people don't consider is that plastic is lightweight and easily blows out of landfills and into our oceans, forests, and beaches where they can harm or even kill animals.

Everything you do, big or small, matters. Still not convinced? Fourteen plastic bags contain enough petroleum to drive a vehicle one mile, but it takes 12 million barrels of oil to produce the plastic bags that Americans consume every year. Of the billions of bags used every year worldwide, four billion become litter.

Small changes in conscious effort make big impacts, folks. And that brings me to principle number four: How can you support others that live and work to produce eco-friendly and sustainable products, communities and lifestyles?

This means taking the time to actively seek out connections with individuals who are passionate about the environment, their communities and the people they serve, and supporting them to create a more sustainable lifecycle. This step can sometimes be the most challenging. To live in and support a sustainable community and economy you may have to sacrifice a few conveniences that you are used to and work a little harder to get to the end result.

For example, I recall when I was a kid we used to pass the grocery store which was just down the road from our house, and drive to the end of town to meet with our local meat and dairy farmer. Tex, as he was known, had been a part of our family for as long as I could remember.

Every year mom would buy about 400 pounds of beef, or a whole cow, which would last us an entire year. In addition, she'd also buy some pork, maybe some chicken, and Tex also supplied us with eggs and milk. More often than not Tex would swing by the house every couple of weeks to drop off the eggs and milk but it was this relationship with our local farmer that proved to be the most rewarding.

This kept our footprint very small: We knew where our meat and dairy was coming from and we never had to worry about the quality because Tex's operation was small.

Get to know your local suppliers. Your dollar is your vote and every time you support your local farmer, butcher, local handmade shop, or local supplier, you create a sustainable lifecycle that's supportive and rewarding for everyone involved.

That's what eco-friendly living looks like. If you simply start by saying no to plastic and yes to reusable bags, that matters. As I started easing into more sustainable practices as an adult, it was learning the facts that made me eager to make a difference. Mama Earth is a gift and she should be treated like the Queen that she is, rather than a dumping ground for our bad habits.

"

Sustainability Is Not Something You Do, It's Something You Become

Amanda Gates

Chapter 2

Radical eco thoughts

1

Where can you turn down unnecessary items? Plastic bags,
to-go containers, bottled water, straws, promo items?

2

How many things do you already own
that could fill your day-to-day needs?

3

How many things do you consume on a daily basis?
Jot down what you buy for the next week.

4

Of those items consumed, what could be eliminated?

Radical eco thoughts

Notes:

Radical eco thoughts

Notes:

THREE

SEEING GREEN: SIMPLE SOLUTIONS START AT HOME

I STARTED my journey back into more eco-friendly practices six years ago. I mention this because nothing is done overnight, and if you're completely new to being eco-friendly I don't want you to feel overwhelmed as you read this book.

Even though I grew up with a bona fide hippie that did sustainable things way before it was cool, it's still a process getting back into the groove of things, and it will be for you too whether you've done it before or are brand new to it.

I had gone rogue for several years and things were far worse now than when Mom and I were doing it back in the eighties, and it was easy to get overwhelmed from it all. My first baby step was becoming a vegetarian. I am a huge animal activist and was sick and tired of seeing how animals were mistreated and abused for the sake of a broken food system.

Animal farming negatively impacts our environment from unsustainable farming practices. It requires massive amounts of land, food, energy, and water plus it causes immense animal suffering. In addition, animal farming causes massive habitat loss, soil erosion and degradation. New studies in the last decade show that big agriculture is causing climate change, massive deforestation, genetic engineering, irrigation problems, and soil pollutants that are affecting our drinking water and oceans, not to mention insurmountable waste.

Reducing what is produced and what is consumed is what it will take to reduce the amount of impact generated. Now I'm not saying that everyone needs to run out and become a vegetarian or even a vegan. Some will argue that being a vegetarian isn't enough because we still consume dairy. But I disagree. Everything matters. Your dollar equals your vote, so make conscious decisions every day that reduce consumption.

The shocking truth about cutting back on meat:

If every American went vegetarian for just one day **we'd save:**

- 100 billion gallons of water, enough to supply all the homes in New England for almost 4 months;
- 1.5 billion pounds of crops otherwise fed to livestock, enough to feed the state of New Mexico for more than a year;
- 70 million gallons of gas, enough to fuel all the cars of Canada and Mexico combined with plenty to spare;
- 3 million acres of land, an area more than twice the size of Delaware;
- 33 tons of antibiotics.

If everyone went vegetarian just for one day, **the U.S. would prevent:**

- Greenhouse gas emissions equivalent to 1.2 million tons of CO2, as much as produced by all of France;
- 3 million tons of soil erosion and $70 million in resulting economic damages;
- 4.5 million tons of animal excrement;
- Almost 7 tons of ammonia emissions, a major air pollutant.[1]

 According to Environmental Defense, if every American skipped one meal of chicken per week and substituted vegetarian foods instead, the carbon dioxide savings would be the same as taking more than half a million cars off of U.S. roads. See how easy it is to make an impact?
Kathy Freston, HuffPost

I lived a vegetarian lifestyle for close to six months before diving into other sustainable practices. From there I moved on to sustainable clothing practices like shopping at thrift stores or swapping clothes, started making my own all-natural cleaners, eliminated toxic air-fresheners, and adopted herbal medicines for everyday illnesses.

When it comes to living an eco-friendly life it's imperative that you approach it with a new perspective. You aren't sacrificing but rather nurturing and shifting the paradigm to the correct way of being. After the industrial revolution we were all duped into thinking that in order to be happy we needed more stuff.

Slick guys on Madison Avenue piqued consumer desire and demand through glossy ads and inexpensive products that made our lives appear easier. Mass marketing campaigns that swept the nation became a global industry all its own and manufacturers realized they would have to keep us coming back for more to keep the money rolling in. Without us realizing it, we became a brand commodity.

Now, after fifty strong years of being marketed to, it's engrained in us that our lives need to be easier, faster and more convenient. We've also drank the Kool-Aid that our products need to be new, so the disposable mindset was born. We've become a culture of pure desire buying with an indescribable sense of urgency for fear of missing out, hyper spending on and consuming things we don't need.

The good news is, there is a way out, simple solutions that are easy to implement start at home. Adopting the idea that having more does not actually give you fulfillment but helping out, giving back and creating change does. Here are 11 quick solutions that start at home.

* By reducing what you consume you immediately reduce the amount of waste that is generated. Learn to reuse items instead of disposing. Recycle items like aluminum cans, plastic, paper, and glass, all of which can be made into a new item.

* Be mindful of how you use water in your home. Conserve both water and electricity where you can. Easy tips like turning off lights when not in use, fixing leaks, properly insulating your home, utilizing daylight instead of electricity, installing energy efficient windows and appliances, and using energy efficient gadgets everywhere you can to reduce your daily energy consumption at home.

* Due to massive deforestation it's imperative that we plant more trees. If you have a home with property, plant trees. They give us oxygen, fruits, calm our energy systems, prevent soil erosion, control floods, and provide shelter to wildlife.

* Be cognizant of your DIY projects. We all want beautiful homes but not at the sacrifice of our planet. Hazardous waste materials like paint, oil, ammonia and other toxic chemical solutions should never be disposed of on the ground. This hurts our water table and our wildlife. I would also go as far as switching out all your home cleaners to all-natural versions. Those toxic cleaning chemicals are not only hurting you and your family, but when they get washed down the drain, they end up in our water table too.

* Probably one of greatest, and loudest gestures I've made to be green was to take the Drive Less Walk More campaign to extreme. In 2011 I decided to get rid of my car for one year as an experiment to see if I could get around without it. Not only was I able to get around easily, but I saved a ton of money and started walking more. (And I should mention this was before Uber became a thing. In fact, Uber did not hit my suburb until late 2015.) It's now been seven years and my experiment's still going strong. It has been a simple, yet effective way

to live an eco-friendly life. If you're afraid to give up your car or can't, learn to take public transportation for your daily commuting needs or try carpooling with your office colleagues to save fuel and reduce your carbon footprint. If your office is a couple miles away from home, I would suggest trying to ride a bicycle to work one or two days a week.

* Another easy tip that I implemented almost immediately after buying my home was to change out all the light bulbs from 100 W halogen bulbs to LED alternatives. Almost every appliance and electrical gadget now comes in an energy efficient model, many with five star energy ratings that consume far less energy than their older counterparts.

> The meat industry causes almost 40% more greenhouse gas emissions than all the world's transportation systems combined. ~ United Nations Report

* The days of the McMansion and being gluttonous with your wealth is over. One of the most eco-friendly things you can do is downsize. This is among the top ways to promote sustainable economics and environmentalism and many young millennials are taking the lead. Buying a smaller house consumes less energy, uses less resources all together, requires less furniture and reduces the amount of things you can consume. You can double down on reducing your carbon footprint by decking it out with goods that are second hand.

* Another super easy tip that you can implement immediately is stopping unwanted mail. So many companies vying for your dollar, destroy the planet by sending you catalogs and junk mail you likely don't read. Opt out from billions of unwanted mailings, simplify your life and save natural resources by visiting www.catalogchoice.org. They offer a free service to opt out of catalogs, coupons, credit card offers, phone books, circulars and more. It helps you to reduce clutter, protect privacy and save the environment. As of the date of writing this book, Catalog Choice had saved:

| 523,504 | 1,091,282.71 lbs | 416,713,640 lbs | 3,641,859,570 gallons |
| Mature Trees | of Greenhouse Gas | Solid Waste | of Water |

* Being a true activist for our environment requires you to take a good hard look at your washing habits. As a culture we wash everything way too much. Not only has science discovered that our obsession with being clean has reduced our natural immune system from building a resistance to diseases, but each person wastes tremendous amounts of water when they bathe, wash dishes, do laundry, or irrigate their garden with city water. Practice taking shorter, fewer showers; wash dishes in a small tub in the sink instead of a dishwasher; cut down on the amount of laundry that you do; and propagate rain water and grey water to care for your garden.

* Start paying attention to the items you consume and the waste they produce. Do everything you can to buy products with less packaging. The excess packaging goes into the trash, ultimately going to landfills which contaminate the environment, harm animals and harm our eco system. You'll learn more about zero-waste living in chapter six.

* Buy as many recycled products as you can. Look for the recycling symbol when you visit the grocery store and make an effort to buy only post-consumer packaging - that will make you environmentally responsible and eco-friendly. Carry grocery shopper bags with you to avoid getting grocery bags you don't need that will later end up in a landfill.

Living an eco-friendly life does have some initial disadvantages. You've become so accustomed to your creature comforts, not paying attention to the fact that it's at the high stakes of our planet. As mentioned earlier, one of the disadvantages is that you may have to forgo some of the modern-day conveniences you've grown accustomed to.

Not many, but conveniences like using paper products, over cleaning and preening, using items laden in packaging, constantly getting new electronics, new clothes, new toys, and over use of your car are types of luxury activities that do little more than create a burden on the environment. One of the best examples is the idea that you need a large SUV to drive around in the city.

While you may realistically need a vehicle, you do not need one that gets poor gas mileage or is made with luxury accessories or advanced electronics that are impractical and consume vital natural resources when made and then disposed of.

Case in point, the Land Rover has a roll over feature that alarms you when you are right side up or upside down. I'm pretty sure you already have this technology built into your brain without a device inside your Land Rover alerting you. It also has a sandstorm feature. While this feature may serve to be useful in Afghanistan, the soccer mom living in Nashville likely doesn't need it.

I propose that the underlying imbalance causing climate change is what I call, "The I'll be happy when syndrome" which is the mistaken belief that you can somehow acquire your way to happiness by consuming more. ~ Emily Fletcher, ZIVA meditation founder, Mindvalley Academy's renowned A-Fest

Four Household Chemicals To Avoid

When it comes to your home, choosing cleaners that are safe and effective is the fastest way to being eco-friendly. Many commercial cleaning products on the market today use harsh chemicals that are not necessary to clean your home and cause damage to you, those around you, and the environment.

If you don't want the hassle of making your own cleaning products, these are the chemicals you need to avoid to keep your family safe.

Here are four major chemicals to avoid that are found in common store-bought cleaners that cause brain fog, joint pain, infertility, cancer and more! These destroy our water table, pollute our drinking water and soil, harm animals and are rarely labeled as highly toxic, even though they are toxic.

PESTICIDES

Many of the disinfectants contained in cleaning products are actually pesticides. They promise to kill household germs but those chemicals contain carcinogens and endocrine disruptors. What most people don't realize is that these ingredients are fat-soluble so once they are ingested it is very difficult to remove them from the human body.

FORMALDEHYDE

Commonly found in nail polish and cheap furniture, this chemical is often used as a preservative and is found in just about every commercial cleaning product on the market because it is a fungicide, bactericide and germicide.

ALKYLPHENOL ETHOXYLATES

Most commonly found in disinfectants, general cleaners and laundry soaps, APE are surfactants which help aid the removal of dirt and grease when combined with water. Like pesticides, they are endocrine disruptors and very harmful to our health.

FRAGRANCES

Fragrance serves little purpose in a commercial cleaner other than concealing the harsh chemical smell and masking odors that create a false sense of cleanliness. Most fragrances contain phthalates, which irritate the respiratory system, triggering allergies, sinus problems and can paralyze our sense of smell.

Household Chemical Alert

Most commercial cleaners do not have to disclose all their ingredients on their label, so you have no idea what products you are putting on your floors, in your toilets or on your counters. This also means you don't know what you are ingesting, breathing in, or absorbing through your skin. DIY home cleaners are an easy alternative to make at home and require little effort.

If making your own seems too hard a task, choose to buy green cleaning products with as few ingredients as possible, and tread lightly: Marketing companies are taking notice of this green movement and creating beautiful natural looking labels that convey "green" or holistic practices when in actuality they contain many of the same ingredients from the same factories, labeled under different names.

It's no secret: Most commercial cleaners at the super market that are geared to help you clean your home are toxic to your health, and to our environment.

Now more than ever, you need to be taking matters into your own hands and making your own cleaning products to keep your home and family safe. Homemade cleaners help you avoid harmful chemicals and they are far more economical too.

Another great perk to making your own cleaning products is that you know exactly what's in them, especially after reading this from Mother Earth Living, March/April issue 2015:

"Conventional cleaning products contain harmful ingredients. In a recent study, the Environmental Working Group tested 21 common cleaning products and identified 457 air pollutants that can be released into the air through normal use. Comet Disinfectant

Powder contained the MOST at 146 contaminants. The study also identified 24 chemicals in cleaning products with well-established links to asthma, cancer, and other health disorders-12 of the chemicals are on California's list of chemicals linked to: birth defects, reproductive problems and cancer"

With a few simple lifestyle changes, you can move toward a greener and healthier lifestyle by using DIY recipes for holistic cleaning. Not only does going green have incredible health benefits, it's affordable too.

Start your green movement by swapping out your toxic, chemical-based cleaning supplies for eco-friendly, DIY alternatives. All you have to do is stock your green cleaning cabinet with the basics, which you'll find in the following pages!

---

1. *Kathy Freston, The breathtaking effects of cutting back on meat | Huffington Post
   https://www.huffingtonpost.com/kathy-freston/the-breathtaking-effects_b_181716.html

Where to Start

Cleaning Green

Get rid of anything store bought: Comet, Soft Scrub, Ajax, Windex, Clorox Wipes - whatever you have get rid of it. Those chemicals are not only hurting your family but are also extremely toxic to your pets, kids and the environment.

Most of us keep these chemicals in a laundry room or worse, under the kitchen sink, creating toxic energy in your home. This is not a healthy home. Buy all-natural safe products and make your own. Here's what you'll need:

- ☑ Baking soda - buy bulk from Costco or online. A large one pound bag will last you a year and it's less than $10 bucks!

- ☑ Borax - buy at your local super market or online. One large box will last you six months to a year.

- ☑ Vinegar - buy bulk from Costco. I generally pick up two to three large bottles. One bottle usually lasts me six weeks, and it's only $3 bucks!

- ☑ Washing soda - can be found online or at your local super market.

- ☑ Essential oils - these can be purchased online or at organic super markets like Whole Foods. Oils to invest in: tea tree, lavender, eucalyptus, peppermint, or lemon. Pick two to three that you like.

- ☑ Castile soap - can be bought online or at any local super market.

Where to Start

Cleaning Green

The ingredients from the last page are all you need to get started in your DIY journey of holistic cleaning. Below are some of my favorite recipes that I use in my own home, but get creative, look online and discover your favorites!

All-Purpose Cleaner

1 tsp Castile Soap
1/4 t eucalyptus oil
3-5 drops tea tree oil
1 T Borax
2 C hot water

Place all ingredients into a spray bottle. Shake and let sit for about 15 min to dissolve and then it's ready to go.

All Natural Scrubby Scrub

1 C baking soda
5 drops tea tree oil
5 drops lemon oil
1/4 C Castile Soap
1 Aspirin

Mix all ingredients together and add a little water to make a paste. Keep in an old shampoo bottle or Mason jar. To use, apply with a sponge and scrub those sinks and toilets clean! Smells good too!

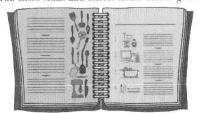

Where to Start

Cleaning Green

All Natural Laundry Soap

1/2 C baking soda
1/2 C powdered Castile Soap
1/4 C washing soda
1/4 C Borax
Add any preferred essential oils

Mix ingredients well. Use 1/2 - 1 cup per load.

The goal with going green is to create a safe and healthy environment for you and your family, along with Mama Earth. When your environment is natural and healthy, your personal energy can become healthy and vibrant. A sick home full of chemicals will show up with a lot of issues, so be mindful in how you care for her and the environment.

Now more than ever it is imperative that we take practical steps to living a simpler, greener life. Make a choice to make better decisions especially when it comes to cleaning. Being intentional with your chores means you'll start living a healthier life and show kindness to Mama Earth. It is not an all or nothing game. It is a matter of small, practical steps that are done in a purposeful way. I first started my green journey by becoming a vegetarian. Then I started making my own cleaning products, and stopped using paper towels. Each year I make larger leaps to live a greener life.

Why do this? It's simple. Not only is it safer for you and your family, but it's saving our planet so your kids have a place to thrive!

"

For every 2 people that use both sides of copy paper at work and home, 2 mature trees are spared annually

Earth 911

Chapter 3

Radical eco thoughts

1
When have you been the most happiest?
Did it involve a thing or an experience?

2
Everything matters, so what simple tips
can you start at home today that will be easy?

3
Do you have the ability to plant more trees? Where can you
turn down paper products to save more trees?

4
What chemicals are in the products you use every day?
What can you replace them with?

Radical eco thoughts

Notes:

Radical eco thoughts

Notes:

FOUR

LET'S TALK ABOUT YOUR FOOTPRINT

IN MY FIRST year of college I learned from my career counselor that I would need four years of chemistry if I were serious about med school. I barely passed chemistry in high school and stoichiometry nearly killed me, but like, how hard could this be? Every Monday and Wednesday I rolled out of bed at 6:30 in the morning to make my 7:00 AM lecture and labs. Chemistry was hard enough when I was well-rested and caffeinated, but these were hardly those kind of times.

As Mrs. Cordoza went on and on about the periodic table, molecules, calculations and I'm sure many other things, I was dozing off or screwing up my lab results. She would always come over to me and my lab partner Tressa and say, "I just don't even understand how you got this result, this isn't even possible!" and all I could think was, "Ummm, you're welcome! Clearly we are geniuses."

Ok, that wasn't the case and I guarantee you twenty years later if you were to speak my name to Mrs. Cordoza she would 1) remember me, and likely not in a good way, and 2) snicker and say, "Oh that child!" in pure exasperation. I'll admit, I was a bit hard on Mrs. Cordoza. Her theories and excitement were totally lost on me because all I really wanted to do was take a nap - that is until my third year in bio-chemistry when we got into carbon.

Carbon is an organic compound found mainly in living things. These organic compounds make up the cells and other structures of organisms and carry out life processes.

Because carbon is the main element in organic compounds, carbon is essential to life on earth. In other words, living things need carbon in order to live, grow, and reproduce.

This finite resource cycles through the earth in many forms making itself available to living organisms so they can survive. Carbon remains in balance through chemical reactions with other elements like hydrogen, oxygen, nitrogen and sulfur found in the atmosphere, and also gets busy with earth herself and bodies of water like ponds and oceans.

Our entire existence is based on carbon; this is the central element to life and without it our planet could not survive. Too much of it and our planet could not survive. These balanced properties of carbon make it the backbone of the organic molecules which form living matter, and to reiterate for those sleeping in the back row, all living organisms are built of carbon compounds. It is the fundamental building block of life and is present in the atmosphere primarily as carbon dioxide (CO_2). And that's where you come in my friend, this thing is called your carbon footprint.

Each and every one of us has the ability to make an impact on our carbon footprint. A carbon footprint is simply the negative impact you personally have on our environment through your everyday behavior. As per the dictionary,

---

A carbon footprint is defined as the total emissions you put out as an individual that ultimately affect CO_2.

For example, the trash you produce, the lights you leave on, the running water you waste, the food you throw out, the clothes you habitually consume, the crude oil you use up combined all impact the personal footprint you leave behind.

Talking about carbon and its importance to our sheer existence was exciting, however, after watching Al Gore preach to us about global warming and watching celebrities run to the nearest Prius dealership to trade in their Porsche 911's, I wasn't sure I wanted to join the revolution. If anything, Al Gore's documentary made me feel helpless and hopeless. The magnitude of it all was just too much to bear. I mean could my two trips to the grocery store with my recycled bags *really* change it? And this is the existential crisis right here: Everyone thinks that they alone can't make a difference, it's too big a crisis to make an impact, and it's someone else's problem.

The good news is that *everything* you do matters. Awareness is key, and you have to start today. Many of the environmental documentaries out there are catastrophic and heart breaking. For me, it's often too much. I sink quickly into despair, and I've realized that's not the answer. Your daily activities matter. Your daily choices matter. Being conscious and intentional with those decisions is what cultivates change. There are many ways to ease into a more eco-friendly lifestyle, and it doesn't have to be difficult to make an impact.

It's time to get familiar with recycle, reuse, repurpose. We are all busy people, but if we just stop and take stock in the little things, we can make a global difference. In 2011, National Geographic published that there are now seven billion people on this planet.

According to World Data:

Between 1900 and 2000, the increase in world population was three times greater than during the entire previous history of humanity—an increase from 1.5 to 6.1 billion in just 100 years!

Now imagine if 10% of that population made a few conscious decisions every day to reduce their carbon footprint and imagine if 25% of that population participated!

Our planet is being brutally abused because life in the twenty-first century has changed immeasurably compared to past centuries. Our lives have become more comfortable, easier and richer than any other time in history. I should also mention that this ease has come at a great cost. We have become fatter, lazier, more fatigued, more stressed, addictions are at an all-time high and, due to an increase in depression, we are more dependent on mood-altering drugs than ever before. We demand instant gratification, seek highs, fear the lows and can't consume fast enough. If you ask me, this sounds like an all night college bender that's fifty years overdue.

In the late eighties the world began living beyond its sustainable means. Twenty years later it was reported by The Living Planet that,

"Humans are using 30% more resources than the Earth can replenish each year, which is leading to deforestation, degraded soils, polluted air and water, and dramatic declines in numbers of fish and other species. As a result, we are running up an ecological debt upwards of $4 trillion dollars."

Essentially, we've taken out a huge credit card, maxed it out and decided not to pay it off. Like gluttonous, irresponsible idiots we've destroyed this planet in the name of progress, protecting only ourselves and our needs, and bitching only about the extreme weather. Instead, we need to be grateful for our Grandmother Earth, and all that She has provided us. It is Her beauty and bounty that most take for granted and will miss when we no longer have it.

The most wholesome path in reversing global warming is radical change: Coming out of the irrefutable bender and rising up as the sagacious humans we are and treating our resources as the gift they are.

So how do we do this and what kind of resources are we talking about? The greatest energy consumption per head on this planet comes from two sources: our home and our travel. And guess what? Both are in your control! So let's get back to our bestie, carbon. Of all the elements on the periodic table, carbon is the most common element for life on earth! From the air we breathe, to the food and crops we grow, to the chemical makeup of our beautiful bodies, carbon is literally the reason we are all here. So if it's so prevalent, why on God's green earth are we so concerned about it?

When we talk about carbon emissions, AKA, the carbon footprint, we're focusing specifically on CO2 or carbon dioxide. CO2 releases into the atmosphere in a ton of different ways naturally; the largest exchange occurring between the oceans and the atmosphere. Animals and humans also emit CO2 through the process of respiration (breathe in oxygen, breathe out CO2).

The cool thing about Mama Earth is that in her own kick ass way, she keeps most of these emissions in balance.

Through photosynthesis, plants absorb CO2, and oceans absorb just about as much CO2 as they produce. Carbon cycles through our air, water, and soil in a continuous process that supports life on earth, and everything is just hunky dory. Wellll, until it wasn't.

Unfortunately, we haven't been abiding by Mama Earth's rules. When we over consume fossil fuels like coal, natural gas, and oil, we release extra carbon and other greenhouse gasses into the atmosphere. And guess what, your bad consumption habits are churning and burning more fossil fuels than ever before.

In addition, we have cutdown large expanses of CO2-absorbing trees to make way for agriculture (be sure to read up on palm oil in the back of this book), housing developments, strip malls and office buildings in the name of progress or we cut down forests to collect lumber to build said developments. By removing forests, we also effectively remove the natural systems that absorb and store carbon, not to mention hurt our wildlife.

Ok, ok. So, you might be glazing over at this point and you're ready to break it off with carbon. Long story short here, CO2 is one of the greenhouse gases that absorbs radiation and prevents heat from escaping our atmosphere. This excess heat is creating higher global temperature average, and disrupted weather patterns which can be seen as devastating fires, hurricanes, tornadoes, tsunamis and rain. If you ask me, Mama Earth is pissed off!

And just to be clear, there are other greenhouse gases too, like nitrogen and methane, for example, but none are as important as carbon. According to the EPA, these other gases only account for about 33% of emissions compared to 65% carbon. So, when you make a hundred unnecessary trips all over town, buy a new outfit every chance you get, leave all your lights on, and use every consumable plastic bag you can, you are single- handedly killing Mama Earth! By adding additional CO_2 to the mix, through your bad habits, nature can no longer pick up the slack.

Enter in the new kid who's exciting and new: planet sequestration. What the hell is planet sequestration? It's literally taking this global warming issue head on and asking you to be responsible until Mama's debt is paid in full. This will be the only way we can offset our carbon overload: by finding ways to negate the carbon that's being emitted.

 Both individuals and businesses can join this revolution and implement energy efficiency, reforestation, and renewable energy programs to start offsetting a portion (or all) of the carbon emissions we've created.

So what's the solution? It's simple. Become aware of your daily habits, decisions and choices. Did you know that the U.S. alone consumes 500 million plastic straws a day? Let me repeat that, in the U.S alone, Americans consume 500 million straws every day!! In Santa Cruz and Monterey counties in California, volunteers pick up 5,000 straws off the beach annually, and that's just two counties. Straws are the most detrimental litter to marine life. Watch one video on YouTube about a straw being removed from a sea turtle's nose and you'll cry for a year and never use a straw again.

On the next page you'll find a fun quick start guide on five ways to immediately reduce your carbon footprint. If you're new to this carbon game take it one step at a time.

Remember it's not an all or nothing game and everything counts.

Your decisions matter and if you think sticking your head in the sand is the best solution, read the article on the next page on [1]Cape Town, South Africa. It's the second largest city in Africa and they just ran out of water. Despite the government telling its residents to conserve, they continued on as they always had ignoring the warnings. Within four short months the entire city ran out of water. If you think this is science fiction, this is only the start of what's to come if we don't start taking our actions seriously.

Walking to your kitchen sink and accessing clean water is a luxury. Taking a shower, using lights and driving a car is a luxury, but it's all at a cost. Now more than ever, we must find every way we can to negate and reverse the damage we've done with smart solutions. Remember your dollar is your vote and your choices and decisions are a vote. You cannot rely on your government or your local authorities for so-called smart solutions because their decisions are often skewed by greed and political agenda. They also don't spend their budget dollars wisely. Case in point, Miami Mayor Philip Levine has approved an unprecedented [2]400 million dollar plan to fight against rising sea levels to protect its boom in high-rise luxury condos. Perhaps, instead of spending 400 million dollars on the symptom, we should instead invest in the actual problem. Just think what could be achieved with 400 million dollars? According to this article, [3]How Many Billionaires Would it Take To Save the World, it turns out we could do quite a lot over the course of five years, so imagine what we could accomplish if we actually all chipped in and tried?

-----

1. Cape Town Water Crisis
   https://www.cnn.com/2018/01/24/africa/cape-town-water-crisis-trnd/index.html
2. Miami Beach's $400 Million Sea Level Plan
   http://www.miaminewtimes.com/news/miami-beachs-400-million-sea-level-rise-plan-is-unprecedented-but-not-everyone-is-sold-8398989
3. How many billionaires would it take to save the planet?
   https://www.bloomberg.com/news/articles/2017-07-27/how-many-billionaires-would-it-take-to-save-the-planet

5 Ways To Immediately Reduce Your
Carbon Footprint

1 Turn off the lights - If you leave a room,
turn off the lights. During the day,
utilize as much natural light as possible
and forgo artificial.

2

Vampire energy - Random cords plugged in all over
the house are charging NOTHING and wasting
valuable energy, not to mention emitting dirty
electricity into your home which causes fatigue and
headaches (computer plugs, cell phone chargers,
drills, iPods...any wireless device that requires a recharge).
All those cords that charge stuff shouldn't
be plugged in when they are not CHARGING.

Showering - Shower one minute less. Put a clock
in your bathroom for one week and determine
how long you typically bathe. A ten minute
shower wastes 5-8 gallons of water. Thats 2200
gallons per person a year! Think of how much
you could save by cutting off an entire minute,
and you will save on your water bill!

3

4 Buy local and buy organic - Food travels an average
of 12,000 miles to get to your local grocery store.
Think of the fuel, crude oil, and resources
necessary to make that happen. If the farmer
down the road has the same product it is a much
healthier option for you and the environment...
and probably tastes better too!!

Eat less meat - Raising animals for food requires
massive amounts of land, food, energy, and water
and causes immense animal suffering.
A staggering 51% of global greenhouse-gas
emissions are caused by animal agriculture.

5

33 Ways I Reduce My Carbon Footprint Every Day And How You Can Too!

- Use 50% consumer products consistently
- Reduced plastic by 90%
- Replaced paper towels with reusable rags
- Replaced paper napkins with cloth napkins
- Sold my car
- Joined a gym less than a mile from my home
- Make all my own cleaners
- I'm a vegetarian
- I repurpose all my glass jars as storage containers
- Have replaced all my toilets with efficient models
- Replaced all my bulbs with efficient LED bulbs
- Light natural fires rather than using central heat
- Eat local organic foods
- Cook from scratch
- Use compostable trash bags
- Use Organic soils for my garden
- Grow herbs and vegetables
- Buy bulk
- Removed dirty electricity from my plugs
- Have a capsule wardrobe
- Buy vintage furniture
- Repurpose glass bottles for water bottles
- Keep lights off
- Stopped unnecessary mail
- Downsized
- Use cat litter made of corn
- Take 2-3 minute showers
- Fill a watering can for the garden with excess water from the kitchen
- Wear clothes several times before washing
- Recycle cooking water in the garden
- Replaced plastic bags with reusable bags
- Replaced all shopping bags with reusable bags
- Recycle, Reduce, Reuse everywhere I can

"

One trillion, one-time-use plastic bags, are used annually and only 5% are ever recycled

EPA

Chapter 4

Radical eco thoughts

1

What does radical change in your daily habits mean to you?
Does it sound doable, scary, unattainable or exciting?

2

What are your biggest fears around living eco-friendly?

3

What would it look like if you adopted five things from this
chapter and started reducing your carbon footprint today?

4

How does it make you feel to know that you are making a
huge difference?

Radical eco thoughts

Notes:

Radical eco thoughts

Notes:

FIVE

THE DEADLY FACTS ABOUT WATER

LIVING A SUSTAINABLE LIFE SEEMS COMPLICATED, right? The word sustainable in and of itself conjures up thoughts of complexity and effort. Well here's the rub: if you think these small acts are too much a burden, guess what your life will be like without running water?

Since most of you have had fresh, clean, running water your entire life, you've likely taken this limited resource for granted. Despite easy access via your kitchen and bathrooms, the reality is it's a finite resource that's going extinct. Even though water is recycled through the earth's natural cycle, people are consuming it faster than Mama Earth can replenish it. Combine that with increased heat from climate change and now our lakes and rivers are drying up. Cape Town, South Africa, which I mentioned in the previous chapter, is experiencing this very thing. So what does all of this mean for you? It's simple: you need to take steps to reduce water consumption and save as much water as possible. In some areas of the world, people don't even have access to fresh water due to contamination. For the rest of us who not only have easy access to it, but fresh clean options, it's imperative to take steps to limit our use of water to avoid waste.

In addition to saving the planet, there are also immense benefits to conserving water. It takes an enormous amount of energy and resources to get water to your home, so conserving means not only saving the planet from enormous stress and demand but saving money; minimizing pollution; reducing the need for costly new wastewater treatment facilities; maintaining a healthy, thriving aquatic environment; and saving energy used to pump, heat, and treat water to get it to your home.

Conserving water is something that we all should be doing and yet no one even thinks about it. We take water and water supply coming into our homes for granted despite the fact that we've created such a high demand for it. Very little of the earth's natural water can actually be used for human consumption. Even though 70 percent of the world is covered by water, there's only about 2 percent that's consumable, and of that 2 percent only 1 percent of it is actually accessible. The rest is saline and ocean-based.

In order for it to come out of your tap as it does, it requires energy pumps, lab testing, treatment centers, sanitary systems, irrigation supply centers, cooling towers and a lot of energy and resources. Producing fresh, safe water is costly, consumes enormous amounts of energy and taps into the limited supplies of water available that you likely waste.

By conserving water, you help drop the demand which also saves money, manpower, earth pollution and a myriad of other resources.

Water is by and far our most precious resource. Considering that we all need water to survive, isn't it strange that many of us have no problem dumping out an old glass of water or wasting water while we brush our teeth, but we support a government that has no problem going to war over oil? Which, let's remember, is producing many of our eco problems mentioned in this book. Once again, think about what would happen if we prioritized our dollars into smart solutions that we could actually accomplish?

Water scarcity is not only caused by a lack of investment in more economic infrastructures and new technologies but also a lack of education around human capacity to satisfy an unreasonable demand for water that is dangerous, if not fatal. One quarter of the world's population is affected by economic water scarcity. Once again, this may sound like science fiction, but within a few short years this could be everyone's reality if swift action isn't taken.

Listen. Everything talked about in this book is important in order to save our planet, but nothing is more important than the topic of water. Our bodies are 60 percent water, so without it the average human body can only survive a few days. [1]It's estimated by the World Wildlife Organization that two-thirds of the world's population will be facing massive water shortages in less than seven years. [2]Around 43 countries already suffer from water scarcity today, and within the next decade 1.8 billion people will be living in regions without water. Many of our water systems are stressed, and every day more and more lakes, rivers and aquifers are drying up or becoming too polluted to use. With altering patterns of weather producing high temps, more and more shortages continue to produce devastating droughts for humans, further destroying precious ecosystems, and making some species close to extinct.

Global warming requires everyone to move beyond temporary drought measures to adopt permanent changes to use water more wisely. It's time to prepare for more frequent and persistent periods of limited water supply and conserve everywhere we can as a collective. Trust me when I say your small changes make a big impact, and only by working together can we improve and sustain water for future generations to come. By conserving water, you lighten the demand, save our eco systems and conserve thousands of gallons of precious water each year.

In the following pages, you'll find 19 ways to reduce your water consumption daily.

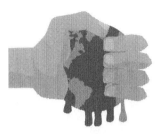

 Our world is changing faster than anyone predicted. Already, freshwater supplies are shrinking, agricultural yields are dropping, our forests are burning, and rising oceans are more acidic—all, in part, due to a warming climate caused by humans. As our natural world changes around us, so should our way of life.
World Wildlife Foundation

19 ways to reduce water consumption daily.

- Turn off the water when brushing your teeth. As much as 130 gallons of water can be saved each month.
- Repair all leaks. Even a small leak, like a dripping faucet, could cause an unnecessary amount of water consumption.
- Stop flushing items down the toilet to dispose of them.
- Avoid wasting water by washing only half of a load. When washing clothes, make sure that you are washing full loads of laundry, when washing dishes make sure the dishwasher is full.
- Take shorter showers.
- Reuse cooking water for the garden. Plants love pasta and veggie water as long as it doesn't have too much salt in it.

- Harvest rainwater for the lawn and garden. My patio is only 200 square feet and I have 2, fifty gallon rain barrels.
- Use brooms or other tools to clean gutters instead of the hose.
- Use a layer of mulch around your plants so they retain moisture for a longer period.
- Use only one drinking glass for your water for the day.
- Cook with water left over in a drinking glass or use it in the garden.
- Install water efficient toilets that flush 3-4 gallons less water than their older counterparts.
- Wash your car less or use a commercial facility that uses less water.
- Reuse towels several times before washing.
- Wear clothes several times before washing.
- Install water saving devices like low-flow shower heads and aerated faucet heads.
- Use fewer plates and dishes or reuse the same dishes throughout the day.
- Don't let water go down the drain while you are waiting for temperature to adjust when taking a bath. Save the water for cooking or the garden or filter and drink.
- Buy energy efficient appliances. An efficient laundry machine saves 18 gallons per load.

---

1. Water scarcity https://www.worldwildlife.org/threats/water-scarcity
2. Water scarcity http://www.un.org/waterforlifedecade/scarcity.shtml

"

Grief and regret is
a place none
of us know until
we reach it

Joan Didion

Chapter 5

Radical eco thoughts

1

How many gallons of water do you use monthly?
Look at your bill and write it down.

2

What are your daily habits around water right now?

- In the morning

- Throughout the day

- In the evening

3

Implement 1 to 3 things from this chapter for the next 30 days.
How much water can you save?

4

What comes up when you hear the term, water scarcity?
How would this change your life, and what steps
could you be doing today to save this precious resource?

Radical eco thoughts

Notes:

Radical eco thoughts

Notes:

SIX

HOW TO EASE INTO ZERO-WASTE LIVING

EVERY SUMMER, I travel seven hours to visit mom and dad at Lake of the Ozarks. They dreamed of someday owning a home on the lake where they could spend their summers, and in 2007 that dream came true!

Surprisingly, many of the people in the area produce trash and throw it right into the lake. Soda cans, wrappers, food scraps and more, all tossed into the lake with little to no regard.

To most, the idea of producing zero-waste isn't even on their radar. With so many other things consuming our attention spans, few have even thought about the amount of packaging and waste they go through each day.

Our on-demand and instant gratification lifestyles swathed in all things pretty and perfect have led us down a dangerous path that's hardly sustainable. As I wrote this I received a note from an Amazon customer who received a clock from our store:

Hello there, I am contacting you because my recent purchase from you was damaged upon arrival. The item was labeled as new when purchased but was clearly repackaged and broken. I would

appreciate a prepaid return label and full refund, or a replacement product please. Thank you so much for your time.
-- Sarah

Now there was nothing wrong with the product - in fact the item itself was brand new - but as a green company we make every effort to not only use as little packaging as possible but repurpose the packaging we do use. This has been our model for years, but because this item arrived imperfect, and seemingly used, the packaging was repurposed, Miss Sarah conveyed that her item was damaged goods.

I find this disposable mindset discouraging, and it falls in line with a recent quote I saw by Terri Swearingin:

"We are living on this planet as if we have another one to go to."

Luckily, Miss Sarah received a kind response from me about the importance of living green; why we must all pitch in to reuse, repurpose and recycle; and despite first impressions, she shouldn't judge a book by its cover.

I not only refunded her money but gave her the clock for free in hopes that she'd realize that even though the packaging wasn't pretty, her new, undamaged clock was exactly what she ordered.

Zero-waste living means you're making every possible effort to reduce landfill-bound trash to a minimum amount. One such example we discussed was plastic bags and plastic straws that litter our planet, so adopting a zero-waste lifestyle is a worthy goal considering that a plastic bag can take up to 1,000 years to decompose in a landfill.

Just take a brief moment to review your own trash and you'll probably find all sorts of things that can be recycled, reused or repurposed.

The idea of a zero-waste lifestyle is not about eliminating every single scrap of trash out of your life, but rather a modern movement that aims at shifting from a linear economy, which is how we are currently doing things and is unsustainable, to a circular economy.

 It's more or less a shift in your awareness about how much trash you actually produce each day and if that trash can become repurposed again and again. A linear system requires a lot of time, energy, effort and cost that ends up in a landfill decomposing for hundreds of years and harming our planet.

Many people live with a disposable mindset and have become completely disassociated from their waste habits and convinced that in order to be happy they just need to consume more, but out of sight does not mean out of planet.

Our landfills are at an impasse, our oceans are filled with five trillion pieces of litter and there are billions of tons of non-recyclable waste that won't break down for hundreds of years. We even have trash floating in space with old, inactive satellites still orbiting earth. As a society, we are at a tipping point if we want to safeguard the future of our ecosystems and humankind.

At its core, a zero-waste lifestyle challenges us to evaluate how we consume, what our trashy habits are, and how those habits are negatively impacting the environment. In this day and age, convenience for the sake of cheap plastics, non-recyclable materials, and disposable products has become the name of our modern ways, but it's detrimental to our planet's health, humans and animal species across the globe. It's time we all change course in how we live. It's not hard, it just requires a little hard work.

Zero-waste seeks to combat the disposable mindset by returning to a more simple and sustainable way of life like the one our grandparents lived. The zero-waste movement isn't something you try but something you do every day. It's about finding friendship with imperfection and striving to get as close to '0' as possible to minimize our trashy habits.

I remember when my grandmother used to bake a cake she would wrap it in beautiful fabric scraps and place it in a used tin. Packaging was not required, because as grandpa would agree, it was the cake that truly mattered, something Miss Sarah from Amazon and many other over consuming humans need to learn. Whether that means a 1%

reduction in output or 99% reduction in trash output, every percentage point counts. Many of us will never come close to reaching zero, but awareness is key.

I encourage all of you to take a moment and peruse the contents of your trash. While this may seem gross, it's a sure-fire way to come face-to-face with how much trash you produce. So many of us are so far removed from the reality of our habits.

In fact, most people think they throw out just a few things when in actuality most people produce an astounding four pounds of land-fill-bound trash every single day according to the EPA. For the average family of four, that's a daily output of more than 17 pounds of trash, resulting in an annual total of more than 6,200 pounds a year!

The cool thing is, even if you've never heard this term before or simply glazed over it, as you get more passionate about zero-waste living, you'll reprioritize how you shop and pay closer attention to packaging or goods you bring into your home. Whether you're an experienced zero-waster or a beginner, there's always something to learn or ways to improve.

At the end of the day, a zero-waste life-style begins with a willingness to change your daily consumption habits and invest in a society built on community, sustainability, ethics, and transparency.

Choosing to be proactive and conscientious of the waste you produce is a step in the right direction to creating a circular economy that protects and restores this beautiful place we all call home.

9 Ways To Ease Into Zero-Waste Living

1

Ditch plastic bags. Use reusable produce bags, lunch bags, sandwich bags and canvas shoppers

2

Repurpose glass. Glass can be used for all sorts of things and won't leach toxic chemicals into your liquids. They are also easy to clean!

3

Eliminate disposable paper products where you can. Instead use bulk rags, cloth napkins, handkerchiefs and buy recycled greener products.

4

Buy Bulk. Every store has a bulk isle. Better yet, shop at places like Costco. It's cheaper and you produce less waste. For example, buy ONE large container of yogurt and divvy it up into those repurposed glass jars we mentioned above.

9 Ways To Ease Into Zero-Waste Living

5 Make homemade cleaners. Commercial cleaners
are filled with toxins, bad for you
and the environment. Buy bulk baking soda and
vinegar. It cleans better, is safer and costs hundreds
less. I can usually get 18 months
out of one large baking soda bag.

6 Eliminate air fresheners. They are highly, highly
toxic, and have been banned in most European
countries. Opt for a more natural option,
like incense.

7 Buy products that are
50% + post-consumer
product.

8 Reuse paper grocery bags over
plastic trash bags. Plastic trash
bags and large contractor bags sit
in landfills for years and harm
our environment. Instead opt for
grocery and yard bags made of
post-consumer paper.

9 Buy used clothes
and furniture. It's made
better and you have an
excellent idea of how it
will hold up!

55 Ways To Live Zero-Waste

- Monitor your trash output. If you don't know how much trash you are producing you can't change it.
- Bring jars with you when you shop to eliminate packaging.
- Compost kitchen scraps: Fruit and vegetable parts, eggshells, coffee grounds, unbleached paper, tea bags, and houseplants.
- Repair all of your goods. Rather than tossing out that ripped jacket or the toaster that won't heat, have them repaired!
- Say no to one-time use items like straws. There is a waste-free alternative for all one-time use items and your choices are a vote.
- Join the refill revolution and refill anything that comes in a bottle. You can refill laundry detergent, dish or hand soap, personal body care items, household cleaning products, and so much more. Find a local co-op or bulk store in your area where you can do this.
- Make more things yourself. The more stuff you make, the less trash you produce. For example, you can make your own toothpaste, body moisturizer, laundry detergent, cleaning products, dressings, etc.
- Buy used products without packaging. New purchases come with lots of new packaging.
- Create weekly meal plans to avoid food waste.
- Learn to borrow or swap items from locals, friends, neighbors and family.
- Install a rainwater system to collect rain to water the garden.
- Repair and care for your shoes to make them last longer.
- Line dry your clothes to avoid using the dryer.
- Bring your own mug to the coffee shop to avoid using a disposable cup, or ask for a real cup.
- Start using all-natural sunscreen with zinc to avoid coral bleaching.
- Buy tree-free toilet paper.
- Reuse shower water by placing a bucket in the shower to reclaim the water and use to flush a toilet or water the garden.
- Stop wrapping gifts in paper and opt for reusable fabric scraps or tins.
- Use a french press for making coffee at home.
- Ask for your receipts to be emailed rather than printed.
- Swap tea bags for loose leaf tea.
- Stop using plastic kitchen bags and opt for compostable bags.
- Stop over using toiletries laden with chemicals and packaging.
- When entertaining, plate the food directly from the oven or cooktop and avoid using serve ware.
- Use drought tolerant plants that require less watering.

Zero-Waste Living

- Buy quality, buy once. Repairing is important to living a zero-waste lifestyle, but you can prevent having to repair your stuff by buying quality products. Get out of the disposable mindset.
- Take care of your things. Do everything you can to make your stuff last longer by using it correctly and taking good care of it.
- Bring your own containers for leftovers when eating out.
- Swap your plastic toothbrush for a bamboo toothbrush.
- Turn old sheets and towels into handkerchiefs, rags, napkins, and cloth produce bags.
- Choose items that can have multiple uses, like Mason jars. They are great for meal prep, baking, canning, cups, and dry good storage.
- Avoid washing clothes regularly and only wash when you have a full load.
- Use bar soap rather than liquid soap. It comes with less packaging that's easy to recycle, and helps you avoid using plastic.
- Continue using old technology like phones rather than upgrading every two years.
- Buy good quality organic soil and mulch for your garden to prevent soil pollution and chemical laden run off.
- Buy organic or use all-natural fertilizers
- Make your own bug sprays.
- Stop using aerosol cans.
- Drive an economic car and plan your trips.
- Eat out less.
- Refuse to use straws.
- Recycle paper and print on both sides.
- Recycle items correctly, and don't throw away cords, cell phones, print cartridges, printers, etc. Dispose of them properly. (See chapter 7)
- Make your own cleaners.
- Buy kitchenware, bakeware and dishes at the thrift store.
- Buy used furniture.
- Turn off lights when not in use.
- Reduce, reuse, repurpose, recycle everything.
- Always use a reusable water glass/water container.
- Get a library card or buy books digitally.
- Learn to package and preserve food so it lasts longer.
- Repurpose wine bottles to water the garden.
- Stop over buying plastic toys for kids.
- Invest in a capsule wardrobe and stop buying clothes every season .

"

If 18 Families said
No to Paper Towels
for one year, 17 Trees
would be spared in
less than a year

The Paperless Project

Chapter 6

Radical eco thoughts

1

How many one use items do you use every day? Straws, paper plates, paper towels, plastic utensils, razors, water bottles, solo cups? What three can you eliminate starting today?

2

On average, for new things consumed, what are your items packaged with?
50% post consumer product, 80% or 100%?

3

How easy would it be to go paperless for 1 month? How easy would it be to eliminate 80% or your plastic consumption?

4

What local thrift and second hand stores are in your area?

Radical eco thoughts

Notes:

Radical eco thoughts

Notes:

SEVEN

RANDOM ACTS OF SUSTAINABILITY

THE ACT of living a sustainable life is one of discipline and responsibility. In less than 100 years, we have placed an enormous burden of stress upon this beautiful place we all call home, and we must change our ways. As humans it is our civic duty to create a balance in which we can live out our dreams while simultaneously being able to coexist in accord to the natural rhythms without harm. It's a simple process; create a circular economy where all things used can be used again and again. As I write this I think back to my Mom in the eighties getting over 25 uses out of a single Mason jar and demanding that strangers pick up after themselves. Mom was such a trailblazer.

The on-demand culture of instant gratification and the more is more for the sake of more lifestyle for so called ease and convenience is both self-serving and self-sabotaging. Our future is in question based on today's present decisions. The single most important task of the day should not be updating your Facebook feed or getting consumed with that seemingly important work project but rather conscious awareness of your daily habits. The very idea that we have to protect the planet and be environmentalists is as alarming as it is narcissistic. We should want to be one with our Mother Earth and instead it causes the great divide, those who are in and those who are out. As Pollyanna as it sounds, I want to exist in a place that doesn't need copious amounts of activism due to a largely intelligent species trashing it.

Our priorities are all screwed up. We consume for the sake of consuming and drive useless dollars and energy to fight wars over commodities that in the end don't stop world hunger, fix the water crisis or solve climate change. We are at a tipping point. How can you deliberately fight on the planet's behalf today?

She's 4.6 billion years old and holds ubiquitous wisdom, deep beauty and a language all Her own and She deserves our every waking thought. The average human lifespan is 77 years of age. Compared to her, we are but a mere speck of dust and yet doing quite a bit of damage.

So many people that I talk to about climate change and global warming think it's someone else's problem, that someone else with more reach, more influence, more power, more intelligence, more willpower, or more money can bear the task. I created this chapter in hopes of planting a seed that change and hope start with you. Not only do your dollar equal your vote, but so does your conscious, everyday decisions about the not so obvious stuff in our lives.

It's easy to hop online and read an article on 'Three Easy Ways to go Eco Today". You may even be graced and persuaded by a stunning write up in the Post on simple things you can do today like turn off your lights, take shorter showers and use reusable bags. These tips are as sexy as they are trendy, and many rush to join the revolution only to forget a mere two days later. Unfortunately, this is where the rubber meets the road.

You no longer have the luxury to be lazy or forget. As you begin doing basic eco practices, you will be faced with lack of motivation, lack of time, and be too tired, and before you know it you'll sink back into your old habits. It's important to remember that being eco-friendly isn't just something you do but something you become. This is a lifestyle that everyone must adopt. This is important because as more and more things get shoved your way, it'll be up to you to stay the course and stay green. What you tolerate and stand for is literally what's under your feet every day, Mama Earth. It's a shame that more people don't update their tree status. Here at the Gates compound not only are our trees a part of the family, but every year we add new members. They are referred to by their first names, honored and cherished, and all of my daily decisions start with them.

Using less packaging, reducing paper products, and washing your clothes less are all great places to start, but what will you do when faced with an incidental crayon, old DVD or printer that no longer is in use? You're entering into the big leagues my friend. Out of sight does not mean out of planet, so will you be willing to go the extra mile? There is no such thing as "away". As Mrs. Parker used to say in AP English, "Amanda, it's somewhere." Some food for thought: that water bottle you drank out of five-ten-twenty years ago is still on this planet *somewhere*.

The good news is, if you incorporate all the tidbits from this book on a regular basis you will gain a love affair with your fellow home and work diligently at keeping her clean.

Intention gives the pain of change a purpose. Setting forth those little goals and achieving them will set you up for success when it comes to what I call Random Acts of Sustainability.

There will be times when you are faced with choosing the easy road or choosing the sustainable road. It's not hard but it does require hard, intentional work to dispose of and recycle goods properly. Following this section you will find a list of random acts of sustainability. I encourage you to continue growing this list.

Every day we are faced with random things that require a more insightful decision that you may not have thought of. I was recently faced with what to do with my old Brother printer. We had paid to have it repaired numerous times, bought additional parts, worked closely with the Brother factory support center and after five years could no longer get any life out of it.

It killed me to have to get rid of it, and yet many products are not built to last in hopes that you'll buy again, a place card for the disposable mindset to grab your dollar again and again, all rooted from greed. Most won't work this hard to get their things to work. With the first sign of ill health, most are running out to replace their device with something new.

Be intentional with your intentions. Let me say that again: be intentional with your eco-intentions. Buy quality products that last so you aren't faced with how to dispose of them in a few short years. Never throw something in the trash for sheer convenience or effort or worse, a lack of concern. If you must buy a new product refer back to chapter two and reread the four basic principles of being eco: What is the expected lifespan? How will you take care of it to get more life out of it?

Many consumers today live with more wealth than at any other time in our history, but never have homeowners been more disconnected from their things and how to care for them. If you buy a home and fail to maintain it properly each year you cannot expect it to perform optimally. Wow, kind of like Mama Earth, right? Care, maintenance, desire and need must all be taken into consideration.

If you truly no longer need your VCR or old DVDs, look at all the alternatives to dispose of them properly. When your cell plan is up for renewal, do you really need a new phone or is yours working just fine? Who cares if you don't have the new time machine built into your phone with teleportation - ok I might be woo'd by that too - but you catch my drift. We have been sold a bill of goods that comes down to this: you'll never get enough of what won't satisfy you and those things you surround yourself with will not fulfill you.

Be mindful in your actions, make it the first and last thing you do, and only then can you be radical in your sustainable habits. That brings me to the idea of useless purchases; because we are living in more affluent times, people are sucked into buying stuff that's used only a few times before being consigned to the basement, attic or junk drawer. Some of these things are pricey to buy, some will be quickly outdated or soon-to-be obsolete and most if not all of it you just don't need to begin with. Bottled water, specialty food gadgets, excess toys, knickknacks, designer clothes, the latest and greatest technologies, whatever it is, you don't need it. Most of the things you already have will do the trick, and if they don't, look into renting or borrowing said item you think you need.

Tackling over-consumption, not over-population will be the key to ensuring sustainable development moving into the future, according to a new report from Christian Aid. The average person in the states uses 176 gallons of water a day, 700 gallons per family, while the average family in Africa uses a total of five gallons for an entire household. The average household in the UK uses over 1000 gallons of water a day, making that country one of the biggest water consumers in the world. They also emit 10.7 million tons of CO_2 annually, compared to only 1.7 million tons for the average family in Africa.

Overconsumption by rich people and the middle class is the main cause of climate change and other global environment crises. Blaming increased population simply diverts attention from where it's desperately needed, which is reining in the runaway consumption habits and addictions of our spending habits. We need to transform and change how we view our economics to make them sustainable and more balanced. Seventy percent of the world's population makes less than $10K a year, but it's the remaining 30% causing all the problems.

The sad thing is that many of the lower economic classes strive to be like the 30%. They are all aspiring to a high-consumption lifestyle because they have been led to believe that leads to happiness and a rich life, but as we all know we cannot sustain the level of demand currently placed on our natural resources without consequences, no amount of *things* makes us happy.

As I write this, my hands are stained in coffee. This morning I peeled apart my eco coffee pods that have a small ring of plastic at the top of the pod. They are made from plant based renewable resources and contain just a small ring around the top rim for stability. After a tutorial from my friend Deborah, I peeled apart the used pod and placed the used coffee in the garden, placed the paper and mesh in the recycle bin and extracted the small plastic ring to place in the plastic recycle bin, a small act that over time will make a big impact. This is a random act of sustainability. Are you willing to change your lifestyle to honor our earth in this way, and take that extra step to make a difference? Everything you do matters!

Choosing to donate old clothes, furniture, or maybe some small kitchen appliances to places like Goodwill or the Salvation Army is easy. But wouldn't it be great, if you could put the more random items that have been sitting around your home to better use?

The following, are how you can start participating in Random Acts of Sustainability to Save Our Planet and become consciously aware of the things you donate to be intentional with your eco intentions.

Random Acts of Sustainability

APPLE will take back any Apple product for free recycling. Apple gives gift cards in exchange for technology that is in good condition to be resold. This reuse and recycling program includes all Apple products https://www.apple.com/shop/help/recycle

Art Supplies - Provides art access to underserved children. A Nonprofit encouraging children to express themselves creatively, and follow their artistic dreams. Your gifts help them provide art & music supplies http://dreamingzebra.org

Books - Donate to your public library

Books - Promising Pages is a nonprofit organization that inspires underserved children to achieve their dreams by becoming bookworms. They provide ownership of books to underserved children and cultivate a lifelong love of reading promisingpages.org

Books - Prison Book Program mails books to people in prison to support their educational, vocational and personal development and to help them avoid returning to prison after their release prisonbookprogram.org

Books - Our Mission is to provide an ongoing source of books to underserved children throughout New Jersey in order to support the development of literacy skills and encourage a love of readingbridgeofbooksfoundation.org

Books - Operation Paperback is a national, non-profit organization, whose volunteers collect gently-used books and send them to American troops overseas, as well as veterans and military families here at home operationpaperback.org

Bras - Bosom Buddies Program - donates bras to shelters and developing nations. Ignite a 'Bra-volution' to decrease the number of bras entering our landfills, while providing substantial social benefits to women and girls in need. https://www.brarecycling.com

Brita Water Filters - Eliminating the Idea of Waste® by recycling the "non-recyclable." Whether it's coffee capsules from your home, pens from a school, or plastic gloves, TerraCycle can collect and recycle almost any form of waste https://www.terracycle.com/en-US/

Cars, Boats, RVs, etc. - Junk my Car lets you sell your junker easily and quickly, absolutely free of charge. Even unusable they can be recycled https://www.junkmycar.com

Cell phones for troops -Cell Phones For Soldiers is a national nonprofit organization dedicated to serving troops and veterans with free communication services and emergency funding. Refurbishes old phones for soldiers https://www.cellphonesforsoldiers.com

Cell phones for charities - Recycling for Charities is a Recycling Organization that allows individuals an opportunity to recycle cellular phones, PDA's, Palm Pilots, digital cameras, and iPods http://www.recyclingforcharities.com/index.php

Cell phones - How to recycle your phone no matter where you live https://www.popsci.com/recycle-your-phone

Cell phones - Provides phones to survivors of domestic violence, and provides domestic violence victims the opportunity to call for help while reducing their carbon footprint http://www.verizon.com/about/responsibility/domestic-violence-prevention

Cell phone -- By donating your old cellphone, someone is given a LifeStraw®, which provides 700 liters of safe drinking water, about one year's worth. It removes 99.9999% of waterborne bacteria and 98% of waterborne viruses http://www.lifecellproject.org

Cleaners - How to safely dispose of your home cleaners with low environmental impact in mind https://www.earth911.com/inspire/programs-initiatives/safety-dispose-cleaning-products/

Cleaners - It's all about choices and doing what's best for the environment: How to Dispose of Household Cleaning Products Safely http://www.healthycleaning101.org/how-to-dispose-of-household-cleaning-products-safely/

Clothing - A youth run organization founded by teens focused on helping teens in need. No child deserves to struggle, whether homeless, cold or hungry. Committed to helping teens in through clothing donations, and supplies http://threadsofcare.org

Clothing - Collect and recyclse textiles to protect the environment, reduce waste, and increase the efficient use of vital resources http://www.planetaid.org

Clothing - Donation Town is the internet's best resource for donating clothing and other household goods to charity http://www.donationtown.org

Computers - Strives to expand access to technology in the developing world https://worldcomputerexchange.org

Construction Materials - Cabinets, doors, sinks, toilets, paint, etc Habitat for Humanity takes it all http://www.habitatforhumanity.org

Corks - Drop off at Whole Foods

Corks - Inspiring a negative carbon future, closed loop manufacturing. ReCORK. is North America's largest natural wine cork recycling program https://recork.org

Craft supplies - Items for creative use their mission is to inspire creativity, increase access to the arts through affordability, and encourage reuse http://www.lancastercreativereuse.org/directory-creative-reuse-centers.html

Crayons - The CRAYON RECYCLE PROGRAM takes unwanted, rejected, broken crayons to a better place, where they will be recycled into new crayons https://www.crazycrayons.com

Diapers - (Unused diapers) works to meet the basic needs of all children and families living in the United States so that all babies remain clean. dry and healthy http://www.diaperbanknetwork.org

DVDs - Gives to sick children, veterans and others in need. is a charitable organization that aims to bring video game consoles and games to sick children in hospitals getwellgamers.org

DVDs - Gives to veterans. Their mission is to provide entertainment to Vets who are unable to obtain movies on their own dvds4vets.org

Everything Else - A grassroots and entirely nonprofit movement of people who are giving (and getting) stuff for free in their own towns. It's all about reuse and keeping good stuff out of landfills https://www.freecycle.org

Eyeglasses - Brings eye exams and glasses to the 1.1 billion people in the world who lack access to vision care. Lenscrafters. Pearle Vision, Sears, Target, Lion's Club http://www.onesight.org

Foreign coins and notes - You can donate unused U.S. and foreign currencies to help UNICEF in its mission to put children first https://www.unicefusa.org/supporters/organizations/companies/american-airlines/change-good

Formalwear: Prom & Bridal Dresses national network bringing together local dress drive organizations to help girls find out where they can donate their used dresses or get a free dress donated to them http://www.donatemydress.org

Formalwear: Brides Across America offers free wedding dresses for military & first responder brides http://www.bridesacrossamerica.com

Formalwear: Prom & Bridal Dresses - Where kindly donated dresses are made affordable for others and also help support breast cancer causes bridesagainstbreastcancer.org

"

In only 50 years we have consumed more resources than in any other time in history.

The Guardian

Chapter 7

Radical eco thoughts

1
What things do you no longer need that can be
donated intentionally?

2
Intention gives the pain of change a purpose.
What feelings come up when you think about donating your
items more purposefully, and freeing up your space?

3
How can you use your abundance in a more positive way and
give back to your community?

Radical eco thoughts

Notes:

Radical eco thoughts

Notes:

EIGHT

SEEING GREEN: HOW TO BRING IT ALL TOGETHER
AS A LIFESTYLE

LIVING a sustainable life every day ensures that we will have and continue to have plenty of water, materials, and resources to protect our environment and human well-being. Sustainability is a simple principle, and yet so many of us want to make it a complex issue smothered in excuses, lack of time, convenience or absence of know how. In her book about the loss and grief around her daughter, Quintana, Joan Didion writes,

> *"In theory our mementos should bring back the moment, but in fact, they only make clear how inadequately we appreciated the moment when it happened. Grief is a place that none of us know until we reach it."*

Everything that we require for our survival and well-being depends directly or indirectly on our ability to nurture our natural environment today. That being said, this is not an "I'll do it tomorrow," decision. Being a steward of sustainable practices today creates conditions under which humans and nature can coexist in harmony while simultaneously fulfilling the social, economic and other requirements necessary for our future generations.

When I think back to those foolish years with mom, my youthful mind was full of hope and excess. I didn't want to see mom as a pioneer but rather as the hippie that stood out fighting for a cause that seemed gratuitous and pointless. Looking back, I realize that mom single-handedly spearheaded a movement that none of us appreciated until now, a place that none of us know until we reach it. If we continue at our current rate, we will realize how much we should have appreciated the beauty and bounty around us. And if we all chip in like mom does, we certainly can.

I remember mom standing in our 100-year-old farm house canning peaches and plums, making jams and jellies, pickling cucumbers and tomatoes all from the harvest that year. Literally down to our skivvies, mom with her long blonde hair up in her vintage 1940's hair clip (which she still has and wears today), she and I would have two box fans blowing through the kitchen's summer heat while playing Merle Haggard in the background. The rewards that nature would provide us would be plenty. Not only would we have a sufficient amount for winter, but plenty to gift to friends and neighbors.

We would head down to Tex's farm and stock the freezer with our winter's meat, fill up the cellar with our canned goods and dad would usually sneak a few bottles of homemade beer or moonshine in the back of the shed that he thought mom didn't know about. Mom would then head to the back of the shed, grab the beer and make beer biscuits from dads stash of hooch. Those are some of the sweetest memories I have and some of the most joyous. Through those memories of working together, building community and enjoying earth's bounty, we found great fulfillment because we used everything we had and did it together.

No matter what your level of interest, your actions matter. Remember your dollars and decisions equal a vote. Saying no to straws, saying no to excess packaging, using what you have, and being responsible with your consumption habits are all important steps in the right direction. Conserving your resources like energy and water consciously and taking care of our environment as best as you can, creates healthy and fair communities.

By simply paying attention to your day to day actions and being present, you will see opportunities arise that equal a sustainable decision. For example, the other day I went to the restaurant Chipotle to get lunch for me and a friend. Instead of having them place our items within one of their to-go paper bags, I brought my own canvas shopper. A seemingly small insignificant choice. However, the average Chipotle gets over 500 customers per day. If by reading this book we could convince even a quarter of Chipotle's customers (a very conservative number) to decline the extra bag, 875 paper bags would be spared in only one week!

On a grander scale, they'd save 3500 bags a month and over 42,000 bags a year. And let's not forget, that's just ONE store with a conservative number of customers saying no. If we could get the message across to all 2250 stores nationwide, we just saved 94 million paper bags in one year. Let's just say that's a lot of trees! Man, mom would be so proud!

As I mentioned in Chapter 1, even if you can't do twenty things every day this is an opportunity to learn how to adopt maybe three to five easy, everyday practices that matter. As mom said, this idea that it's an all or nothing game is nonsense. Your one little thing does matter and becoming aware of your gluttonous consumption habits allows you to say no to consuming unsustainable resources. Imagine if the government paid less attention to oil and more attention to the resources in our backyard. Perhaps instead of having Presidents Day we could have, 'say no to meat day', 'say no to grain day', 'say no to plastic day'...you get the idea. There are over 300 million citizens living in the US alone. If we could get even 75 million to adopt these practices of doing one thing nationally every day that would create quite an impact, not to mention quite a stir!

Another seemingly small choice is saying no to plastic. Yes, yes, this has all been drilled into us before, and I'm not saying anything to you that you don't already know. However, did you know that glass can be recycled endlessly into new bottles or new products over and over again without any loss in quality? This is important to consider when not all plastics are treated equally. Did you know that yogurt cups, hummus tubs, shampoo bottles, medicine bottles, some microwave-safe take-out containers or cottage cheese containers are made with #5 plastics? What is that you say? If you're trying to be more eco-conscious by recycling your plastics, most facilities won't take the #5 or polypropylene made containers. Unlike it's #1 and #2 counterparts, #5 polypropylene has a high melting point, and so they are much harder to recycle. It is gradually becoming more accepted by recyclers, but why not avoid them all together, especially considering that few plastics produced are actually recycled and quality can be quite temperamental unlike its glass counterpart.

This is why getting educated on your recycling habits matters. There are so many alternatives to using plastic. Just think if we could get those 75 million people on board with saying no! While there are alternatives to oil and gas, there is no alternative to water. If we continue to say yes to plastic, we are agreeing to 80% of said plastic going into our oceans and killing our marine life, not to mention leaching chemicals into our soil and water table.

Bottom line, pay attention to your decisions. Being an environmentalist sounds fancy but what it comes down to is finding ways to live more sustainably every day by using resources in a way that maintains their regeneration for the future.

Being sustainable and eco-friendly doesn't mean living without luxuries but rather being aware of your consumption habits and reducing unnecessary waste like the Chipotle bag or straws. Wouldn't it be grand to live in harmony with this beautiful place we call home without having to constantly defend and protect her? To live amongst humans that honor and respect her?

This is not a trendy thing that only hippies do. While it has become a media blitz campaign to, you guessed it, sell more products, bottom line to remember is, your decisions equal a vote. Remember, to be eco-friendly you have to be mindful of your day-to-day choices because it's arguably the most important task on your to-do list today. To avoid greenwashing or overwhelm, refer back to the four simple principles from chapter 2:

1) How can I reduce my day-to-day consumption habits?

2) Do my consumption items have a low environmental impact?

3) How can I reduce my carbon footprint?

4) How can I build strong community around an eco-friendly life?

Small everyday decisions add up. We've consumed more crap in the last 100 years than in any other time in history, all in an effort to find happiness. We are no longer living in harmony with our planet but rather mooching off of her resources and getting angry at her weather patterns and rising sea levels. We have essentially become irate three-year-olds, and yet we are considered the most intelligent species on the planet.

What does being eco-friendly look like? Not the monk, not the hippie it looks like you.

Eco-friendly is the everyday mom or dad, kid or college student, making conscious decisions throughout their busy day, every damn day. You will have days that are more complicated than others, but I promise the tips in this book are both tangible and doable. Life fluctuates, ebbs and flows. But your consumption habits waste, destroy and use up what we need for the sake of what we don't need. Who do you know that you could get on board with this ideology? Perhaps instead of gifting them with a piece of useless technology or an unneeded widget, you start gifting recycled canvas shopper bags or produce bags, give a gift card to your local farm, bake food from local ingredients, make homemade laundry soap or house cleaners provided from chapter three or give more intentionally with usefulness in mind.

Living an eco-friendly life is not something one does but rather something you become. This is a lifestyle. It doesn't look like inconvenience but a way of life to ensure our future generations have a home. Plus, it just feels darn good. When I leave the grocery store with my 15 reusable shopping and produce bags, I know that I am making a difference. When I hand over my glass container to the deli department for some delicious mock chicken salad or grilled sweet potatoes, they are happy and encouraging to take my container, which lights me up.

Reusing what is produced and what is consumed is what it will take to reduce our impact generated. We consume over 25% of the world's energy and resources despite only accounting for 5% of the population. The cool thing is, almost 80% of our unsustainable practices start at home, which is within our control. Trees are an incredible resource that many take for granted. Even if you have a tiny patio or garden, plant trees. I worked closely with a local horticulturist in my area to learn how to plant trees in containers for my patio. I'm the proud mama of four trees, Edgar, Arthur, Astrid and Gladys. They are family members that are cared for and honored.

As an advanced Feng Shui practitioner, I am a huge advocate for our homes and their importance to our health and well-being but beautiful energy is what creates a beautiful home which ultimately starts by creating harmony with your place card on this earth. How you care for your home and treat her matters. Updating your home is important to her Ch'i or energy and yours, however, be cognizant of your DIY projects. Beautiful homes are ones that blend harmoniously with the environment. This is the perfect yin yang of life. But throwing paint out improperly, dumping toxic chemicals into the ground which later hit our streams or dumping chemicals down the drain is not being a steward for our planet.

Install energy efficient bulbs. The initial cost may be high, but having done this myself five years ago, not only have we seen a monthly reduction in our electric bill, but our output of energy has been greatly reduced.

Whether you decide to go vegetarian for a day, grab all your excess water, eliminate paper products, refuse plastic, or reduce junk mail, all these decisions are easy to implement and make an immediate impact. Again, this is about creating a paradigm shift in how you view sustainability. This isn't something you do but something you become.

Trust me when I say that if we don't start taking radical action, we will be faced by radical consequences. Imagine having to drive to the local square to attain your allotted five gallons of water for the day or quite possibly the week! We can survive without oil, but we cannot survive without water. Cape Town, South Africa, is just one example of global warming causing extreme drought which has affected its residents greatly. Sure, we don't know what we are capable of until we

HAVE TO do something, but do you really want to be faced with living off of five gallons of water a day?

Rather, wouldn't it be easier to conserve today, cut back and soften our current demand to maintain our lifestyle? I'm sure Cape Town residents are wishing they had taken it more seriously. For them, gone are the days of water conveniently coming out of the tap or shower head. This is just the start if radical change doesn't occur.

It takes an enormous amount of resources, energy and manpower to get water to your home. Since most of us have always had this luxury, we don't even consider it a finite resource. It will just continue to magically appear out of the tap, right? We are consuming faster than Mama Earth can replenish it and now with extreme droughts, lakes, reservoirs and rivers are drying up. Remember only 1% of earth's water is even accessible. If you live in an area with plenty of water you may say to yourself, well we will be fine in our city, we get 50% precipitation a year. Well that's what many have said here in Nashville until a massive increase in population occurred in the last ten years. Many new occupants are from Texas and California, where drought is of major concern. Demand is demand and if we consume faster than Mama Earth can replenish we are all susceptible to lack of resource. Conserve, conserve, conserve! Collect rain water where you can and be cognizant of your demand.

Water is no longer a temporary measure but a permanent shift in mindset in how we use it. Reuse pasta and cooking water for the garden (plants love it), use a rainwater barrel to recollect the natural resources, take shorter showers, flush less, and grab every drop you can to repurpose. Again, just think of the impact if those 75 million citizens thought this way.

This may seem extreme, but this is becoming everyone's new reality. To many people, thinking this way isn't even on their radar. I mean who has the time, right? Well, if we're having to walk down to the local square because cars are prohibited, and water no longer comes out of the tap, funny how we'll make time. It will suddenly become our reality and we'll wish for the days of ease and less restriction. If only we had taken this eco stuff more seriously! From water to consumables to plastic to packaging, everything matters.

Being a mindful environmentalist doesn't mean giving up your luxuries but rather being aware of our resource consumption and reducing unnecessary waste. Trust me, our perception of "luxury" will change if we lose the basics like water. I remember growing up my mom had this gigantic metal razor with a real diamond blade and fancy carved handle. I thought nothing of it until I was older and realized it was my great grandmothers razor from the thirties. My grandparents never dreamed of things like single-use razors, forks, cups, bags, or food storage containers, but these days, you can find a plastic alternative to almost any object and then throw it away after only one use. Many of the environmental issues today stem from toxins released into the environment by trash and the inability of that trash to actually break down, not to mention the fact that marine life and land animals eat it. When you make a purchase, consider the item's life expectancy. How many times can the item be used?

My mom still uses my grandma's razor to this day. The diamond blade can be sharpened, and she has never once considered using a plastic, few time use, razor.

One item that has gotten over 88 years of use and has never once touched a landfill. What a concept.

Ask yourself numerous times, what is the environmental impact of this object? What is the environmental impact of this choice I am about to make? It's not so much that people aren't willing to do the work, it's more the fact that people are just not paying attention. Most are not present in their day-to-day actions. You may be physically brushing your teeth as the water goes down the drain but cognitively you are already in today's meeting or thinking about the 25 things that need to get done by this weekend.

This brings me back to our obsession with consumption for the sake of happiness. What if instead of getting whipped up in a froth over the seemingly important tasks of the day, we focused on one thing and did that one thing well? Many of the harsh decisions we make are not for lack of trying but lack of a good mindset. We are unhappy, stressed, anxious, sad, frustrated and disappointed. In my world, this is called Below the Cross Emotions™. We cannot make good decisions from this state of mind because stress and anxiety change how we weigh risk and reward.

In order to develop a rich relationship with Mama Earth, we must come to it from a desire to do the work in a loving way, not from martyrdom. Seeing it as a risk, it's time consuming, it's too hard, I don't know how, rather than viewing it as a reward, will stop us from seeing the benefits of what it will afford us and future generations. Our biggest and only task of the day is how we can live in harmony with the environment around us, but if we are too busy and whipped in a froth of stress, life will pass us by and we'll wonder how in the heck we got to a place where living without water, trash pickup, and electric homes is the norm.

Too many of us focus and stress about the wrong things. Perhaps instead of updating our Facebook status it's time to update our tree status, to rekindle our love affair with nature. Now to some this may not come naturally. However, I am addicted to nature and have been known to accost her when I am in a forest. Spending just 30 minutes outside can revitalize a tired brain and uplift our spirits. Walking in the grass or enjoying a picnic with your family outside can be one of the most joyous, free adventures that feeds your soul.

Blinded By Science, a book by author Matthew Silverstone, proves that trees impart positive health impacts on things like depression, concentration levels, stress, and some forms of mental illness.

Matt also found that spending time in nature and near trees, as well as hugging them, relieved headaches. Numerous studies in children have shown significant psychological and physiological improvement in their health and well-being when they're involved with the outdoors. Research has also showed that children function better and are more creative when in natural, green environments. Activities outdoors are positive mood boosters for both adults and children and require nothing but your time. If it's free and makes you happy, what more could ask for?

I am in love with Mother Nature. Everyone needs to learn the art of lighting the spark that lays dormant within themselves to help save this precious jewel. The art of being a steward for this planet is no longer just for the few caring souls, but for the millions who want this planet to thrive. Living a sustainable life is one of discipline and responsibility. At the current rate we are going our planet will run out of resources due to the burden we have placed on her in less than 100 years. As humans it is our civic duty to coexist in accord to nature's natural rhythms. Our on-demand culture and desire for instant gratification is no longer serving us. It's time to get back to basics, and maybe hug a few trees. Take a photo of it and send it to us. I would love to know your #TreeStatus.

Send us your #TreeStatus
LetsGetEco@TheGatesCompany.com

This is no longer someone else's problem or something to do tomorrow. This is today's dilemma that everyone needs to start pitching in to help with. This isn't the grade school science project where the smart kid does all the work and the rest of us take credit for it. There are no gold stars, there's no such thing as extra credit. This isn't a sliding scale, it's pass or fail, and currently we are getting a major fail. We need to lessen our burden, be mindful of every action we take, and all contribute.

This book includes a plethora of resources to create a sustainable home, reduce your carbon footprint, and ways to ease into zero-waste living along with random acts of sustainability. I encourage all of you to add to these lists. Continue being pioneers in sustainable practices and forging on in harmony with our planet. Encourage those around you to chip in, help them, teach them and be stewards within their own communities. How can you chip in? How can you encourage and empower those around you, neighbors and family, to change their habits? Be a leader of change and know that you are well equipped for the task at hand.

Our planet is precious and has given us so much. It is time we return the favor, get off the fifty-year bender and start treating her with the love and respect she deserves.

Be kind, be generous and love Mama Earth like the wise grandmother she is.

> ❝
>
> 4 Billion Starbucks to-go cups are thrown away annually, and most go into landfills due to the plastic lining. Since 1985 they've rewarded customers with a discount if they bring in personal tumblers.

Eco Watch / Starbucks Co.

Chapter 8

Radical eco thoughts

1
What are some of your favorite ways to spend time in nature?

2
How can you teach and empower others to get them excited
about being eco-friendly?

3
What one thing brings you the most pleasure about nature?

4
How has nature changed your life?
What gifts does she provide you every day?

Radical eco thoughts

Notes:

Radical eco thoughts

Notes:

NINE

ADDITIONAL RESOURCES TO BE A SUSTAINABLE ROCK STAR

WE ARE ONLY as good as our resources, including but not limited to the people who are willing to step up and lean in to an eco-friendly life. As a culture we are anxious and restless because we no longer hold the pursuit of a common ideal. But by approaching eco persistently and lovingly, we can create a healthy, balanced eco system that allows our Mama Earth to thrive and give us a common ideal worthy of fighting for. We have to because it's necessary to our survival.

Moving towards a balanced, sustainable life gives us purpose. Through the collective, we can save humanity and bring equilibrium back through a circular, balanced economy. If you've ever wanted to be a super hero, now's your chance! This not only serves our planet but serves us in meaningful ways. I refuse to accept that people are unwilling to do the work. Yes, becoming eco has become a trend, but despite increased popularity of the terms eco, sustainable, green, environmental or any other you'd prefer to plug in, the possibility that humans can ban together within their societies to create an economically strong circular economy is possible as long as we stop viewing everything as unlimited and impossible. This is absolutely doable folks, so grab your super hero capes!

This book gives you everything you need to get started to improve the quality of life on this planet through a process called sustainability. This is a call to action. What does eco look like? What does activism look like? What does change look like? YOU.

I (insert your name here) will be responsible and proactive in my decisions to minimize the negative impact I have on this planet. I will do everything to maintain balance in my daily actions, while simultaneously being a steward of innovative activities moving forward to care for Mama Earth as she has done for me.

Additional

Resources

Where to Start

Resources

As my friend Beth says, 'it's not hard, it just takes a little hard work.'
Your dollar is your vote. Your choices and everyday decisions are a vote,
so start making conscious, intentional choices everyday.
Below are some additional resources. I call this, *Where to Start to Get Smart*.
And be sure to join our private facebook group, *Mindful Living* where we can
build community.

Plastic Straws 80% of all marine debris found in the ocean is land based, and 80-90% of the marine debris is made from plastic. How can you make a difference by simply saying no to straws? https://thelastplasticstraw.org

Conserving the lands and waters on which all life depends Every acre we protect, every river restored, every species brought back from the brink, begins with you. https://www.nature.org

For decades, **WWF** has engaged with millions of Americans, leading businesses, and government leaders to prepare for inevitable change and reduce the emissions that drive climate change. https://www.worldwildlife.org

#5 Plastics, or high-density polyethylene, are plastics that require a high melting point making it difficult for most recycling facilities to accept them. Yogurt cups, hummus tubs, shampoo bottles, packing materials, are all made of #5 go to www.preserveproducts.com to find recycling centers in your area

Natural Resource Defense Council, United States-based, non-profit international environmental advocacy group. NRDC works to safeguard the earth—its people, its plants and animals, and the natural systems on which all life depends. https://www.nrdc.org

Where to Start

Resources

Where to Start to Get Smart.
And be sure to join our private facebook group. Mindful Living
to build community.

 EWG empowers people to live healthier lives in a healthier environment. With breakthrough research and education, we drive consumer choice and civic action. https://www.ewg.org

 Greenpeace exists because this fragile earth deserves a voice. It needs solutions. It needs change. It needs action https://www.greenpeace.org/archive-international/en/

 Friends of the Earth - If you oppose widespread adoption of nanotechnology, genetically engineered foods, and human gene patenting you'll appreciate their clear stance and advocacy. https://www.foei.org

 Earth Justice - Dedicated, experienced lawyers taking on the underdog fights that many feel too powerless to fight. Donating here is levels the playing field between large corporate interests and the often woefully underfunded voice of our struggling ecosystem. Because the earth needs a good lawyer says it all! EarthJustice.org

 Ocean Conservancy Become a voice for the ocean. Our ocean faces many threats like the onslaught of ocean trash, overfishing and ocean acidification. Ocean Conservancy is developing innovative solutions to save our ocean. https://oceanconservancy.org

 Earth Island Institute - organizes and encourages activism around environmental issues and provides public education. Through fiscal sponsorship, it provides the administrative and organizational framework for more than 50 individual projects. http://www.earthisland.org

Sustainability

sus·tain·a·bil·i·ty

avoidance of the depletion
of natural resources
in order to maintain an
ecological balance

PALM OIL

WHILE WRITING chapter four I went back and forth on whether or not to include the conflict going on around palm oil. Since the book is all about easy ways to lean in to an eco-life, palm oil is typically where I lose people because it is in many of their favorite things. But the more I thought about the devastation surrounding this product, the greed of factories using palm oil, the deforestation of rainforests, loss of entire eco systems and single-handedly killing endangered species like orangutans, I realized that I needed to include it so that you could make an informed decision on your own.

The reason you should avoid palm oil is because the factories using the cheap commodity are burning the rain forests to quickly clear them out and replace them with palm oil plantations. This slash and burn approach is not only wiping out the forest and killing entire eco systems but releasing massive amounts of carbon emissions when they burn.

*There are three tropical forests left in the world, The Amazon, in South America, The Congo in the basin of Africa, and the Southeast Asian rainforest that used to span Indonesia. Eighty percent of the Indonesian forest however, has now been wiped out, with the slash and burn technique, and replaced with palm oil plantations.

These fires are intentionally set because burning the forest is the fastest, cheapest and most profitable method of clearing rather than using heavy equipment. Considered one of the most corrupt governments, officials are paid off so that companies can come in and grow the cheapest vegetable oil in the world. It's in cooking oil and processed foods, cosmetics, and detergents for home cleaning products. It's one of the cheapest commodities produced making companies tremendous, outlandish profits at the sake of the planet, eco systems, animals and air. In 2015, the fires were so bad they emitted more carbon daily than the entire US economy. As fires continue to rage across the forests and peatlands of Indonesia they are on track to pump out more carbon emissions than the U.S.'s entire annual output.

*The deliberate slash and burn fires are illegally started to clear the forest for paper and palm oil production. In addition, the region is currently experiencing a strong El Niño climate phenomenon that's creating drought conditions in Indonesia, exacerbating years of draining of peatlands. Companies destroying forests and draining peatland have made Indonesia's rainforest into a huge carbon bomb. Despite the Indonesian government turning a blind eye because they are being paid off, the destruction is indisputable when half of Asia is living with the consequences.

What can you do? I've said it before and I'll say it again, your decisions and dollars equal a vote. **Stop buying products with palm oil**. Every decision matters and if you stop buying it the demand goes down. Avoid cheap products, processed foods, look at what's in your cleaning products, and buy only cosmetics that don't contain palm oil ingredients.

And pay attention, manufacturers are getting clever and renaming palm oil to hide it.

Alternate Names for Palm Oil

- Cetyl Alcohol
- Cetyl Palmitate
- Elaeis Guineensis

- Emulsifiers 422, 430-36, 470-8, 481-3, 493-5
- Glyceryl Sterate
- Octyl Palmitate
- Palm Kernel Oil
- Palm Stearine
- Pamlate/Palmitate
- Palmitic Acid
- Palmityl Alcohol
- Palmolein
- SodiumDodecyl Sulfate
- Sodium Kemelate
- Sodium Laureth Laurel Sulphate
- Sodium Lauryl Lactylate
- Sodium Lauryl
- Suloacetate Sterate
- Steareth 2 and 20
- Stearic Acid
- Vegetable Glycerin
- Vegetable oil
- Vitamin A Palmitate
- Anything with the word "palm"

50% of all packaged food contains palm oil. Buying products made with palm oil encourages manufacturers to continue to wipe out forests, eco systems, and harm animals for the sake of bigger profits.

Here are just a few:

- Bagel Bites
- Balance Bar
- Ben and Jerry's
- Bertoli
- Bird's Eye
- Blue Bonnet
- Boston Market
- Butterball
- Cadbury

- Canada Dry
- Cheez its
- Chef Boyardee
- Classico
- Clif Bar
- Country Crock
- Dr Pepper
- Earth Balance
- Egg Beaters
- Fleischmann's
- French's Mustard
- Girl Scout Cookies
- Gulden's Mustard
- Harmony Trail Mix
- Hawaiian Punch
- Heinz baby food
- Heinz Ketchup
- Hellmans
- Hunts
- Jack Daniels
- Jiffy Pop
- Keebler
- Kellogs
- Knorr
- Knott's Berry Farm
- Kraft
- La Choy
- Lea and Perrins
- Libby's
- Lipton
- Little Debbie
- Luna Bar
- McDonald's
- Mott's
- Mrs. Fields
- Nabisco

- Nutella
- Oreo
- PAM
- Parkay
- Pepperidge Farms

Earth Resolutions
One year to get
eco clear

Your Earth Resolutions Start Today!

Jot down your Earth Resolutions. What will you accomplish over
the next year?

What do you hope to accomplish?

How will your daily actions make a big difference to you?

And how will making a difference impact *your* life?

Use a scrap piece of paper

and place it on your refrigerator or mirror.

res·o·lu·tion

Your Earth Resolutions Start Today!

What does eco-friendly look like?

You!

Easy, Everyday Habits to be More
Eco-Friendly

1

Turn off the water when brushing your teeth today. You just saved 130 gallons of water this month! Boom!

2

Use one drinking glass for today, like a Yeti, tumbler or repurposed glass bottle. Keep it up and you just saved $500 annually.

3

Use fewer plates and dishes throughout the day and reuse the ones you do use. You just saved 20% output on energy and water! Whoo hoo!

4

Reduce your shower to four to five minutes daily. You just saved sixteen gallons of water today! Keep it up, and save 5,840 gallons for the year.

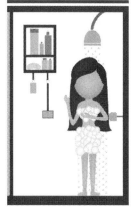

5

Stop flushing items down the toilet to dispose of them as waste. You just saved 5 gallons of water!

Weekly At-A-Glance
Easy, Everyday Habits to be More
Eco-Friendly

1

Monitor your trash output. If you don't know how much trash you are producing you can't change it. For every 4 lbs of waste produced, currently, only 1 pound is recycled. Let's change that!

2

Create weekly meal plans to avoid food waste. On average people who plan save 3 hours a week and $50. Look at you being eco!

3

Reuse clothes and towels several times before washing in the laundry. On average, one load of laundry uses 27 gallons of water. And line dry your clothes which saves 350kw of energy for every two people in the house. Hooray!

4

Avoid wasting water by only washing full loads of laundry. When washing dishes make sure the dishwasher is full too! You just saved 35+ gallons of water for every load that's full.

Good Job!

Monthly At-A-Glance

Easy, Everyday Habits to be More
Eco-Friendly

1

Repair all leaks. Even a small leak, like a dripping faucet, could waste 3000 gallons of water annually; which is what one person uses annually for showering.

2

270,000 trees are killed daily to provide toilet paper globally. Buy tree-free toilet paper, and save trees!

3

Reuse cooking water for the garden. Plants love pasta and veggie water as long as it doesn't have too much salt in it. Harvest rainwater by installing a a rain barrel for the lawn and garden. You just saved 330 gallons this month! What an eco rockstar you are!

4

Repair all of your goods. Rather than tossing out that ripped jacket or the toaster that won't heat, have them repaired!

Easy. Everyday Habits to be More
Eco-Friendly

1

Use a layer of mulch around your plants so they retain moisture for a longer period of time and help protect the soil.

2

Most home improvement projects require tools you'll never use again. Borrow, swap or rent from local, neighbors, family or the local hardware store.

3

Use brooms or other tools to clean out gutters and sidewalks rather than using the hose and wasting water.

4

Only consume products that have multiple uses, like mason jars, shopping bags, glass jars, or reusable boxes. These items can be used all year long and prevent waste, and keep life simple!

Conscious Consumerism
quickstart guide

Air Hair Dryer - This brush is designed to act as a diffuser, drying hair 40% faster. Eco-Friendly, Ultimate Air Dryer Brush, Made with Recycled and Sustainable Materials. http://bit.ly/2K3Vuge

Allbirds - As a certified B Corp, they do business differently. The environment is their number one concern, and how they treat it is just as important as the bottom line. All packaging is recycled too with 90% post-consumer cardboard. https://www.allbirds.com

Eco-friendly razors - BPA free, Triple Razor, 100% recycled #5 plastic and completely recyclable after use. Package is reusable as a travel case and made from renewable wood sources. https://thrivemarket.com/p/preserve-triple-razor-system-handle-and-2-blades

Eco mattress - Avocado, seeks resources that are environmentally-friendly, renewable, recyclable, and always consider environmental factors along with their impact on health when sourcing their materials and manufacturing their products. https://goo.gl/uoHTyG

Eco Mattress - Tuft & Needle Is The First Mattress Ever Certified To Be Free From 300+ Harmful Chemicals. Their Mattress received the UL GREENGUARD GOLD certification, the strictest chemical emissions standards tested for by UL Environment. https://goo.gl/ix9YMZ

Eco Toothbrush - Plant based, Natural Bamboo Toothbrush, Eco-Friendly Biodegradable BPA Free Bristles, eco-friendly, vegan paper based packaging lasts four times longer than plastic counterpart. http://bit.ly/2K1xs5v

General Store - Thrive Market is a membership community that uses the power of direct buying to deliver the world's best healthy food and natural products to it's members at wholesale prices. https://thrivemarket.com/myaisle/

Green Line Copy Paper - creates products from recycled materials. Their multipurpose paper is recycled from paper itself, helping preserve trees. http://greenlinepaper.com/product-category/office-paper-envelopes/multipurpose-paper/

Green Toys - sells toys made from 100% recycled materials — milk jugs being the primary material. They also use plastic recycled from other types of products. Their toys surpass U.S. and international standards for BPA and Phthalates. http://www.greentoys.com

Kitchen Trash Bags - Unni ASTM6400 compost trash bags These trash bags are 100% compostable, meet the stringent requirements of municipal composting programs, and are BPI certified. For reference, they're almost half the price of Glad bags. http://bit.ly/2K4jKyS

Natural All Purpose cleaner - Plant-based formula effectively removes food, soda, juice, grease, oil, sugar, pet accidents, fingerprints, footprints, lipstick, tree sap, grime, plant based, non-toxic. http://bit.ly/2Hh1wYZ

Nebia Shower head - uses 70% less water than a regular shower. The average home saves 20,000 gallons of water per year. http://bit.ly/2Hf5kdq

Pens -Bic pens made of recycled water bottles Made from 86% post-consumer content. Retractable and refillable. http://bit.ly/2J96ebV

Poo Trash Bags - If you have a pooch, you probably go through quite a few waste bags taking him or her on walks. These disposal bags are biodegradable and disposable. https://www.onyalife.com/product/disposal/

Rain Barrel - The best way to conserve water. The rain barrel is one of the oldest and most useful tools in repurposing rain water. http://bit.ly/2JY634t

Reusable Produce bags - reusable produce bags to put your veggies in. https://www.onyalife.com/product/reusable-produce-bag-8pack/

Reusable Produce Bags - Flip and Tumble reusable produce bags. I love these bags! I've had mine for five years and they still work great! http://bit.ly/2HjhfXs

Reusable Sandwich Wrap - Wrap your sandwiches and rolls in reusable sandwich wraps. Made from recycled PET bottles, with a fully foodsafe PEVA lining. https://www.onyalife.com/product/sandwich-wrap/

Reusable Straws - Stainless Steel Drinking Metal Straws by LexStraw with silicone inserts. Perfect For 30/20 oz Yeti & RTIC, Ozark Tumblers and Rambler. http://bit.ly/2K1G24b

Shower timer - Bathroom Shower Clock Timer w/Date, and Temperature. http://bit.ly/2K2mnkL

Solar Charger - Made of eco-friendly silicone rubber and ABS + PC material. #1 best-seller solar charger is an eco-friendly alternative to the traditional rechargeable battery pack. https://amzn.to/2Kz4bSL

Toilet Paper - Stop wiping with trees and start using tree-free toilet paper. Feel good toilet paper that uses 50% of its profits to build toilets. https://us.whogivesacrap.org

Do you know of an amazing eco product not listed? Let us know!
LetsGetEco@TheGatesCompany.com or visit
GatesInteriorDesign.com/LetsChatEco

66

Bic pens have sold over 100 billion disposable pens since 1950. If all those pens were lined up end to end, they would circle the Earth 350 times.

The EPA estimates that Americans throw away 1.6 billion pens Annually.

Recycle your pens,
https://www.terracycle.com

IN CLOSING

WE ARE ALL ENLIGHTENED beings when we are in our true nature, our Tao, but as Peter Matthiessen, author, Buddhist teacher, and naturalist said, "There are lamps that haven't been turned on, all it takes is a little glimpse to turn the lights back on." We are anxious, restless, chaotic, and as each of us goes in seemingly different directions we see and find nothing, but we sense that this source of restlessness, anxiety and chaos is not a strange place, but the feeling of not being home. There is a void, a disconnect within us all to our true nature, our Tao. We get lost in a froth of external things trying to fill that void, to turn the lights back on, but only find more restlessness. Perhaps if we just fill the void with more things, the restlessness will go away, or so we thought.

If we continue to live within fear, defenses, blame, prejudices, oppressions and repressions, we will never be able to intuit the existence of our true nature. Earth and the beauty around us belongs to us all. By showing her that we adore her, we care for her in a responsible way and see glimpses of home. When you rekindle that love affair, you find your soul, you find yourself and suddenly you are living with meaning and purpose. The anxieties, emotions and prejudices can fall away, and the lights can be turned back on to your true nature.

Here, we return to a place and truly see it for the first time. This is home.

Darling,

Remember to pick up after
yourself, and do the best
you can.
You've got this eco stuff!

azaleas,

mom

Who Is

Amanda Gates

Amanda is a professionally trained interior
designer, advanced feng shui practitioner, podcaster and award-
winning blogger. She has been seamlessly marrying interior
design and feng shui for twenty years to help her high-end clients
create designs that are energy aligned™, to give them the home
and life they've always dreamed of.

Interested in learning more? Head on over to our website for
additional resources at gatesinteriordesign.com

WITH LOVE

amanda gates

Printed in Great Britain
by Amazon